KITCHEN ESSENTIALS

THE JOY OF HOME COOKING

GARY MACLEAN

KITCHEN ESSENTIALS
THE JOY OF HOME COOKING

BLACK & WHITE PUBLISHING

First published 2018
by Black & White Publishing Ltd
Nautical House, 104 Commercial Street
Edinburgh, EH6 6NF

1 3 5 7 9 10 8 6 4 2   18 19 20 21

ISBN: 978 1 78530 180 3

Text copyright © Gary Maclean 2018

All photography © Sean Cahill 2018
Except for photography on pages 34, 78, 84, 90, 96, 126
© Gary Maclean 2018

A CIP catalogue record for this book is available from
the British Library.

Layout by Richard Budd Design
Printed and bound by Rotolito, Italy

Foreword by Marcus Wareing

Gary is a very talented chef, and this book is testament to his skillset and knowledge. Having judged Gary throughout *MasterChef: The Professionals* in 2016, he was a very worthy winner. *Kitchen Essentials* is a book that will do as the title says, guide you through the fundamentals of great cookery, from the mastered experience of a true professional. As a cookery college lecturer, Gary is a credit to teaching and education, and has a very firm grip on modern cooking and techniques, as well as his classical repertoire, with a very open-minded approach. Gary has had years to hone his educational training and I am so pleased he has taken the leap to publish it for all to enjoy and learn from.

Marcus Wareing
Founder of two Michelin-starred Marcus, The Gilbert Scott and Tredwells, and one of Britain's most respected and acclaimed chefs and restaurateurs.

CONTENTS

FIRST THINGS FIRST

For this chapter I have thought about all the questions people have asked me over the years on how to get started – the skills and techniques they'll need, what to buy – all of what's needed in a kitchen. It can seem that for many people this is a complete mystery. Firstly in terms of the know-how and secondly in terms of what to buy and how to buy it. There is a whole range of different quality kit available – from equipment that could last a lifetime to something that will fall to bits after a couple of uses. It breaks my heart when I see people spending good money on the wrong stuff – especially because they tend to overspend more often than underspend. I hope to demystify – even if only a little – the best way to practise and develop your kitchen confidence and how to go about kitting out your kitchen. I really believe that the correct skillset and equipment will make your experience of cooking at home a much more pleasurable one.

1

Introduction

So what makes this book different from all the other cookbooks out there in the world?

For a start, I hope you will actually use it – and enjoy it. Many people buy books that look great on a shelf and are fun to flick through, but don't get much day-to-day use out of them. I love to see a cookbook that's a bit messy, been annotated with someone's own notes and generally has that well-loved feel to it. I hope this book will be one of those.

I have been a chef for thirty years in educational settings – and have spent almost that whole time as a student and lecturer. I also taught in a very good cook school for many years. What I have learned during this time, and from the experience of teaching thousands of people, is quite startling. I believe that very few people understand the basics of cookery. What I want to achieve from this is a book that actually works at home. You will not find any MasterChef goings-on, or my high-end restaurant-style food. This book is full of dishes that work at home, using food that is easy to get hold of and relatively quick to prepare and cook.

I have a large family who range from my oldest son, who is now a university graduate, to my youngest two boys, who are just starting out their education in primary school. Throw two teenagers into the mix and what I have found is that cooking at home can be tough.

The time we all eat – what with clubs' different start and finish times and the eighteen-year age gap between my first and last – offers up plenty of challenges for me. I would love to say that we all get around the table and enjoy the same meal at the same time every evening, but as you know, that idealistic vision of the family dinner table is very difficult to achieve, especially when you have kids of different ages and parents who work.

My story of home cooking is not as clear-cut as you might think. I actually had to teach myself how to cook at home – and I know how strange that might sound coming from a chef! For years I was cooking like a chef in my own kitchen;

I cooked like I was in a restaurant. I used every pot, pan and utensil and made a huge mess, not to mention the absolute fortune I spent on food. I had to figure out how to pull it back and keep things much simpler at home. Here's a confession for you: I was so bad at one point that I wouldn't let my wife Sharon into the kitchen until I had cleared up the mess I'd made preparing our family dinner.

So, in essence, *Kitchen Essentials* has been written using my experience as a cook and an educator, but probably the most important skill I have brought to bear is being a father of five and figuring out how best to cook at home.

What your kitchen needs

Having good quality kitchen equipment can make all the difference when cooking at home. The best advice is to build your collection as and when you need to. I have listed below what I think of as compulsory bits of kit. As you develop as a cook your need for equipment will increase as your repertoire expands.

Kitchen knives

Knives are one of the most critical bits of kit that a home cook can purchase. Having a good set of knives to hand can make all the difference to your time in the kitchen. With a bad knife I would struggle doing the most basic tasks. I am amazed at the range of knives that are out there, and the quality – or lack of. I often see home cooks and young professional chefs struggling with the choice and, as with everything, when it comes to knives not buying well is good money down the drain. I use different knives at home than in a commercial kitchen.

Buying knives is not as straightforward as buying the most expensive ones out there. A professional chef will buy knives that'll last for several years of daily use. These can cost anything from £30 for a small paring knife to £150 for a cook's knife. I use German knives; they are kind of old school – heavy, hard wearing and ideal for many hours a day of serious work in a professional kitchen. The downside to this type of knife for the home cook is they are very difficult to maintain and sharpen. A proper understanding of how to sharpen with a sharpening steel is vital to keep the edge on a knife like this.

It is probably easier to advise what knives are best avoided. In my opinion that means anything that has a coloured blade. This style of knife may look the part and match your new kitchen, but as a tool they are hopeless: badly made and designed and normally of very cheap quality. Knife block sets that sell for under £100 are full of knives you will never use and won't be of good quality, even though they are often sold with the words 'professional chef's block'! I have never seen a chef use a block to store knives in my life.

Another thing to watch out for is the word 'Sabatier'. People are under the illusion that if a knife has Sabatier stamped on to it then it's a good one. The reality is that Sabatier is an unprotected name and can be used on anything without repercussion. There are a couple of French manufacturers who make very high quality knives under the Sabatier name, but most Sabatiers are probably best avoided, unless you are paying lots of money.

Advice

Buy knives one at a time. That is, buy what you need – if you buy properly you should only need three or four knives. If you purchase from a good cook shop or department store, take your time, ask to have a hold and feel of the knife, do your research and price check. Another way is to buy online from a professional chef website. Anything mid-range from these suppliers should be a safe bet for home use and you will also save some cash. These sites are good for all small equipment for your kitchen.

Pots and pans

Pots and pans are also an expensive and varied bit of equipment to buy, but as usual it's as simple as *you get what you pay for*. Even so, there are a number of rules you must follow regardless of price.

- Make sure you can place the pot and lid into the oven to a temperature of 160°C-plus. This is crucial for braising and stewing in the oven.

- You need to avoid plastic or rubberised handles.

- Look out for what the pan can be used on. I would make sure it can be used on an induction hob. Even if you don't have an induction hob, the chances are that if you are paying a lot of money for a quality pot or pan it could outlive the hob you have and, when replacing your hob, you should go for induction.

Induction technology

An induction hob is something I started using over twenty years ago. It was a mystery to me back then, as it looks like any electric ceramic-style hob. I admit that using induction takes a little getting used to: the unit will not generate any heat, as induction hobs don't use burners or heating elements underneath the pan. Instead, they employ a series of magnets that excite the iron atoms in a pan to generate heat. The energy transfer to the food is much quicker and more efficient than a traditional electric or gas stove top.

I see people all the time who are still trying to get their heads around the technology. One stumbling block is the misguided perception that you will need to throw out your beloved old pots and pans. The truth is that you might have to buy some new ones, but the easiest way to find out if your pots and pans will work on induction is to see if the bottoms are magnetic. Once you get going on induction you'll be amazed. The speed and control of an induction hob is incredible –

- you can boil a pan of water from cold in a matter of minutes,

- or at the other end of the scale you can melt chocolate directly in the pot with no need for a double boiler.

All the kit you need

Chopping boards I think there is nothing better than a big old wooden board. It feels great when you are chopping and looks good as well, but it's not exactly practical. You can't put it in the dishwasher for a start, and there can be a problem with cross-contamination if you get into the bad habit of using it for everything. On the market today there are loads of chopping board options – from colour-coded to glass. My advice would be to buy a couple of good-sized boards, making sure they fit in the dishwasher. I like the ones that have rubberised edges that stop the board moving.

Graters Graters come in all shapes and sizes, but my best advice is – don't buy a cheap one as it will fall to bits. For me, the best grater on the market is Microplane. I'm not being paid to say this, it's a great bit of kit – ideal for zesting, chocolate, Parmesan – which should last for ages. It's also a good idea to invest in a quality box grater.

Scales I always suggest using digital scales, especially if you are measuring small amounts. When it comes to liquids you can always weigh them too. Measuring jugs aren't always very accurate. When you choose one, I'd suggest a Pyrex jug with a brightly marked scale.

Whisks A whisk is a vital bit of kit – so it's always a good idea to have one or two in your kitchen drawer. If you'd like a whisk that will last, then you do need to spend a little extra cash. Choose one that is fairly robust but with thin wires, and avoid those that are completely coloured.

Bowls A good selection of metal bowls will be of great help in the kitchen. I really like metal bowls as you can get them completely clean and they will last for ever.

Spoons and spatulas I buy ladles, serving spoons, and slotted spoons in one-piece stainless steel. I'm not keen on additional handles, as these trap dirt and burn easily if left in a pot. I love real wooden spoons, but the secret is to buy loads and when they get tatty and burnt throw them away. With spatulas and spoonulas, it's worth spending a bit more on a good make; the cheap ones don't last long.

Strainers and sieves Any kitchen will benefit from a selection of strainers, sieves and colanders. These tools can do loads of jobs from draining vegetables and pasta to sieving flour and straining soups and sauces.

Tubs and storage My main way to store food at home is vacuum packed, so the storage I most need is vacuum bags. All the same, I have loads of tubs, for cooling food, or storing foods that don't vacuum well. Try and buy the same brand so they all stack neatly together, and a tight fitting lid is critical. I also use zip-lock sandwich bags. All these things really help reduce waste and let you use up leftovers properly.

Temperature probe A food temperature probe is a vital bit of kit for the home cook, and they're a lot less expensive nowadays. Once you start to use one, you'll wonder how you got by without one. A temperature probe will really help you get food cooked to the correct temperature, which is brilliant for food safety.

Gadgets Having said all this, I confess I have a problem with gadgets! Don't get me wrong, I love them, but what I don't love is the drawers and cupboards in almost every kitchen I visit that are full of gadgets gathering dust. If you buy a gadget, make sure you actually need it and will use it, because once it ends up in the cupboard the likelihood of it ever seeing the light of day again is slim. The rule is: if you use it, it's no longer a gadget – it's a useful tool.

Food processors I use a variety of different bits of food-processing kit depending on what I am doing. These range from little household hand-blenders with a bowl attachment, to machines costing thousands of pounds. My best advice on food processors is to do your research before buying one – talk to friends who have them and read reviews. You don't need to spend lots of money to get a machine that works for you.

Pasta machine A couple of recipes in the book use fresh pasta. It's doable with a rolling pin, but a pasta machine makes it easier and more fun. I'd suggest spending about £50 on a good-quality Italian one as it will last a long time. Please don't wash the machine in a sink of water: if you do it will never work again. Clean after use with a damp cloth.

Vacuum packer This brilliant little gadget has revolutionised my cooking at home. It doubles the life of your food, saves space in the fridge and if you have to freeze the food it defrosts very quickly because it's flat. They start at about £50 and the only downside is the bags can be expensive. I always think of the huge savings made on food not going in the bin.

Pestle and mortar It's old school and not really a gadget as such, but this is a fantastic addition to any kitchen. It's brilliant for crushing and grinding whole roast spices. Even if you don't use it often it will look amazing on your kitchen windowsill and your neighbours will think you are windswept and interesting . . .

Pressure cooker I just love pressure cooking food. I have two at home that I use every week. But I don't cook in the pressure cooker to save time, rather I use it to capture flavour; for me, the fact that food cooks 70% quicker is a bonus. When I was a kid I was terrified of them – my mum had one, but I can't remember ever eating anything from it. Perhaps she just had it on to scare the kids out of her kitchen. You'll see that I'm always talking about pressure cookers in this book, so be brave – buy yourself one and use it.

Moulie or ricer These two bits of kit do similar jobs. A moulie is more versatile – from sieving soups to making mashed potato. On the other hand, the ricer is simply essential for the best ever mash.

Organising yourself
Getting off autopilot

Planning . . . Sounds boring! I know what you are thinking: who's got time? I bet you can find time to google holidays, cars, shoes – everything but what's for dinner. But this is a serious business. I can think of nothing that will improve your cookery, diet and wallet more than planning. We're all creatures of habit; we do the same stuff over and over again, we buy the same stuff week in and week out without thinking about it. Food is expensive, but if you spend a little time each week planning what you are going to buy you will save a fortune.

Planning meals properly is a change of lifestyle. Certainly, it's a big step in helping you start on the journey of a much more varied diet. Getting home from work and looking in the fridge and thinking *what's for dinner?* never ends well.

I learned how vital the skill of planning was when I was once asked by a national newspaper to write six recipes that would feed a family of four for £30. My first reaction was to refuse the challenge, as I thought £30 would never cover a decent family meal.

I sat for an hour and wrote six varied family dishes, then I made a list and went shopping. When I got to the till, my bill came to £35. I couldn't believe I'd got even close to the £30 mark. It shows how ingrained my chef habits are that I have been known to spend that on an evening meal for one – without any difficulty at all.

Planning also gives you the opportunity to learn new cookery skills, which will inevitably change what you want to cook. The reason for this is you have put some time and effort into meal planning rather than simply shopping on autopilot, as most of us are prone to do.

Food shopping has become a real chore for many people. The reality is that people spend very little time and thought on their weekly food shop – and as a result, many of us work from a list of about ten dishes rotated each week. I think the reason for this is that we tend to shop on the same day each week, in the same shops – we even park in a similar spot in the car park, pick the trolley from the same spot and then go round the supermarket following the same route and picking up the same food. The positive consequence of this is that it's really easy to change what and how you eat by changing how and where you do your shopping.

Essential techniques

Seasoning: taste, taste and taste again

Seasoning is vital in cooking. It's the difference between creating an average plate of food and a brilliant one. I think it's pure habit for a good chef to taste; it happens instinctively. It's a bit like pressing the clutch when changing gear – you do it without thinking. You don't want the people you are cooking for to be the first to taste your food. Remember, too, that you don't always season with salt and pepper; sugar, vinegar and lemon – to name but a few – are things you can use to enhance and balance the food you are cooking.

Essential knife skills

We have all seen the TV chefs showing off and chopping things really fast. In reality, it's more important to cut and chop *properly* rather than quickly. Good technique takes time and lots of practice. You must learn good technique first, and the speed will come naturally with practice.

The first thing you will need is the correct knife for the job.

- It's important to feel comfortable with the knife you have in your hands.

- It also needs to be the correct size; there's no point in dicing a kilo of carrots with a 9 cm paring knife when a 25 cm cook's knife will do the job much more quickly, safely and easily.

The technique a professional chef uses when cutting food is sometimes difficult for beginners to understand. If the person is right handed, then the left hand is used to guide and control the knife. They will do this by making sure the side of the blade is in constant contact with the fingers of the left hand. This is done by tucking in the fingers and thumb; that then exposes the first knuckle, and the first knuckle is then in constant contact with the knife. This makes using a knife much safer and will reduce your chances of cutting yourself.

- The other important technique you need to learn is not to chop, but to slice. You will always find that if the angle of the blade is correct then the food cuts much more easily.

- So, you should never try and drive the knife into the food; instead, slice through using a *pulling back and down motion*, as well as a pushing forward and down motion.

- Different foods will require a slightly different technique – but never chop!

- Always secure your chopping board to make sure it won't slip.

To be blunt the other main reason people cut themselves is because they are using a blunt knife. If your knife is blunt then any cut you may get from it will be much worse than if the knife is sharp. I know that sounds strange – it feels counter-intuitive that a blunt knife will cut you worse than a sharp knife – but this is because when you work with a blunt knife you have to use much more pressure. So, keep your knives sharp!

Food prep

Understanding cookery processes

What is a cookery process? It is a technical term for how your hob, oven and grill – and any other bit of kit you might have in the kitchen – apply heat to food. In this section I am going to explain the main ways we apply heat to food and what happens to the food during this process.

At home you use an array of cookery methods to make food more palatable and digestible, to help in the development of the flavour and to make it safe to eat. Understanding the principles of each cookery process will help in your cooking. Two of these methods are

- moist heat, which is the use of liquids in the cooking, *and*

- dry heat, which is cooking without liquids.

Boiling and simmering

These are simple cookery methods, but I feel they are often misunderstood. The temperature should always be 100°C for both boiling and simmering. Some foods need to be added to cold water and brought up to the boil, and others should go straight into rapidly boiling water. Boiling works very well with cheaper, tougher cuts of meat, root vegetables and greens.

Braising and stewing

Braising and stewing are long slow methods of cookery, which require liquid and a tight-fitting lid.

Stewing can be done both on the hob and in the oven. I feel it's much better to stew in the oven as you have full control of temperature and don't need to keep checking on the food like you do when it is on the hob. The best temperature for stewing is about 140°C. You can turn the temperature up if you are pushed for time, but don't go past 170°C.

If you are stewing on the hob, the temperature of the liquid in the pot should be about 80°C and shouldn't boil. The key thing to remember is that you are trying to keep the contents from boiling; boiling will lose you liquid, so the content will thicken up and could easily burn.

Another way of stewing on the hob is to use a pressure cooker. I love working with them. I think the flavour is much better than using a regular pan and, as it is 70% quicker, it'll save you money on your energy bills. The secret of the pressure cooker is to get it up to pressure as quick as you can and then turn the heat down as low as it will go while still maintaining pressure.

Foods suitable for stewing are chicken legs and thighs, and those diced tougher cuts of meat – the slowness of the cooking process breaks down the tough fibres, making them moist and tender.

Braising is slightly different in that it is always done in the oven. It's almost a cross between roasting and stewing. The food is *partially* covered in liquid and the pot is sealed with a tight-fitting lid; the liquid keeps the exposed food from drying out and the lid traps in the steam.

Foods suitable for braising are larger cuts of meat like bones and rolled shoulder joints.

Steaming

Steaming is a great method of cookery – it's very healthy – but one that's underused in most homes. You can steam by:

- direct contact – that is, the steam comes into contact with the food, *or*

- indirectly in a covered bowl.

The temperature of steam is 100°C, the same as boiling and simmering, but it has much more energy and tends to cook things quickly and precisely. It can also be used as a long and slow method for tougher cuts of meat.

It's perfect for cooking vegetables and fish as you retain much more of the flavour and nutritional value of the food than in boiling, because you are not losing anything in the cooking liquor. Another advantage is that it's a moist heat and there is much less risk of the food drying out.

Deep fat frying

This method of cookery is a very fast and dry method of cookery. The temperature can be anything from 130°C for blanching – i.e. cooking chips from raw in a lower temperature to soften – to a much higher 180°C for crispy golden-brown foods.

Unlike steaming, this method is widely used and is the unhealthiest way to cook.

The theory of what happens to the food in hot oil is that the oil instantly makes a seal around the outside the food. The food is normally coated in something like flour, batter or breadcrumbs, which creates a shell around the food. The food then steams on the inside.

There are some foods that need to be deep-fried – such as battered fish – but anything that has a crumb coating can be brushed in a little oil and oven baked to give you a similar result.

Shallow frying

This is another very fast method of cookery. Tender prime cuts such as steak or chicken are particularly suitable for shallow frying, as is fish. This is especially true of filleted portions – with skin-on fillets you can create that super crisp skin that everyone loves. And loads of vegetables taste fabulous when shallow fried – onions, peppers and mushrooms, blanched and refreshed green vegetables all love to be shallow fried. Remember, too, that stir-frying falls under the banner of shallow frying. Watch out for the following when shallow frying:

1. Always make sure the pan is very hot before adding the food. If the oil is not hot enough the food will stick and absorb the oil.

2. Use a neutral oil such as vegetable, rapeseed or peanut oil. Personally, I never shallow fry in quality oil such as olive or cold pressed rapeseed oil.

3. Often you will see TV chefs shallow frying with butter. This is tricky to get right; butter can't be taken to the same high temperatures as oil and can burn very easily. I tend to do most of the cooking in the hot oil and once I have created the colour and crispness of the food I turn the heat down and add the butter.

Blanching and refreshing

Blanching and refreshing allows you to pre-cook vegetables up to a day ahead of time.

Blanch This word has several different meanings, depending on who's using it and why, so it almost always needs some qualification or explanation. Technically, it means to 'change' or 'set' a green vegetable's colour from flat to vivid green while keeping it, in effect, raw. Some people use blanch to mean 'parboil': to cook a vegetable halfway, then shock it so it can be finished later. For example, chips are often blanched in low temperature oil so that they can be finished quickly (and crisply) in hot oil later. Many cooks use the term to mean plunging a vegetable into heavily salted water that's at a rolling boil, fully cooking that vegetable, then removing it to an ice water bath.

Shock/Refresh To shock means to plunge food into ice water in order to halt the cooking. Green vegetables, such as green beans and broccoli, are commonly boiled in salted water and immediately shocked. This method is useful if you want to prep food in advance of a meal.

To blanch and refresh vegetables

Bring a large pot of lightly salted water to a rolling boil, add the prepared vegetables and cook for a few minutes. The cooking time will depend on the type and size of vegetable being blanched. You're looking for the vegetable to have a slight bite. Remove with a slotted spoon and plunge immediately into ice water. This stops the cooking and will retain both the nutrients and colour.

Blanching and refreshing guidelines

- Cut, trim and peel the vegetables into uniform shapes to promote more even cooking – and nicer presentation!

- Cook vegetables for as short a time as possible to preserve texture.

- Use a large amount of water in comparison to the amount of vegetables, to allow the water to keep boiling.

- After refreshing, drain the vegetables and cover with damp paper towels. Refrigerate until required.

- Reheat them by quickly sautéing in butter, steaming, grilling and dropping back into boiling water for a few seconds, or by re-heating them in the microwave for a minute, covered with cling film and a knob of butter.

- If vegetables are blanched and refreshed properly, they should stay green – even if you like your green vegetables softer.

Browning

If there is one thing that will transform the flavour in your food, it's adding colour to it by browning. I see home cooks automatically turn down the heat as soon as they get a little heat and sizzle in the pan. The reality is that you achieve a great deal of flavour from browning meat. The reaction of colouring meats, breads and all foods that are not primarily sugar-based is called the Maillard reaction. This reaction happens when heat is applied to these foods above 120°C. The bottom line is: brown your meat.

Here's how to brown

1. Test the pan with a little of the food before committing the whole lot. You will know it's hot enough when you get a sizzle coming from the pan. If the sizzle is very noisy and uncomfortable, turn it down; if there is no sizzle you have no heat, so turn it up and wait.

2. Don't put too much food in the pan at the same time. Only put in enough food to cover the base of the pan or pot.

3. Place the food carefully in the pan and once it's in, whatever you do, don't shoogle, shake or stir: this will stop the browning and the likelihood is that the food will be stuck anyway.

4. If you think the food has browned enough, try moving one piece; if it freely comes away from the bottom of the pan it is ready to be turned. Once all the food has been turned, remove it from the pan.

5. If you need to, reheat the pan and brown the remainder of the food.

Baking

Baking is a dry method of cookery. I think it's a brilliant way to cook. The oven is turned to a fixed temperature that ranges from 150°C to 220°C. If you follow the recipe, baking is predictable and consistent; and even better, baking fills the whole house with amazing aromas.

Know your oven

These days most people have fan-assisted ovens. The purpose of the fan is to create an even heat throughout, which means you can use the whole oven. Without a fan, the oven struggles when more than one shelf is used at the same time – if you don't have a fan and are putting more than one tray in then you'll need to up the temperature and adjust the time a little.

Even so, remember that all ovens are slightly different. I recently moved house – where of course I had to work with a new oven – and for about three days I burned everything before I realised what was going on. So if you find that anything oven-baked is cooking faster or slower than I state in the recipe, it will probably do the same for every recipe – the difference is in the ovens we are using.

Roasting

Roasting is very popular offshoot of baking: same oven and temperature, but different rules. For lots of us, there is nothing better than a well roasted chicken or joint of beef sizzling away in the oven from which all the cooking juices can be made into the tastiest gravy or sauce.

A temperature probe is an essential bit of kit when roasting; it ensures you are cooking the food to the correct temperature so that it's is safe to eat and it also gives you confidence to cook the food to the minimum temperature.

The first rule of roasting is to prepare the food properly for the oven. With meat, this is usually done by tying or trussing. The purpose of this is to ensure the food is compact and there are no straggly bits like legs poking out. For example, with a chicken once the legs have been tied or bound with elastic bands they are tight against the narrow part of the breast. This helps the bird cook evenly because the legs protect the narrow end of the breast meat and vice versa. Next you will need to season the meat; if it's a whole animal then season and stuff the cavity with some fresh thyme, garlic and half a lemon.

Make sure you don't cook the meat directly on the tray. Instead, use a metal rack or a bed of root vegetables to keep the meat off the hot tray. The vegetables will taste amazing and will also help stop the meat juices from drying out.

Another important roasting rule is to turn the food. Gravity plays a significant role in creating dry food. If you turn the food regularly it will retain the moisture much better.

Last but not least, rest the meat once it comes out the oven. Resting gives the meat a chance to settle; it evens out the temperature and the inside colour of the meat. If you cut in too early you are left with a big puddle of flavour all over the floor.

Poaching

Poaching, a wet method of cookery, is perhaps the most misunderstood of all the cookery processes. It's a gentle process that needs attention and an understanding of temperature, but if done correctly it can produce some amazing dishes.

The liquids you can use for poaching are endless: ranging from simple vinegary water for poached eggs to red wine for pears, from stock for fish to syrup for fruit. The main rule of poaching is to never let these liquids boil. Before you start, make sure the pot, pan or tray is big enough for the food you want to cook and then skim the liquid as you go.

A few simple things will help with poaching: a slotted spoon to get the food out the liquid, and a cartouche. A cartouche is just a fancy name for a circle of greaseproof paper that is placed directly on top of the liquid: its job is to keep the food submerged and help keep the moisture in.

Grilling

Grilling is a great method of cookery. It's fast and healthier than shallow frying, mainly because the fat falls off as you grill. There are two types of grilling: one from above and the other from below.

Let's look at grilling from above first. This method can be done with great results at home – my only bugbear is it can make a real mess of your oven. To start, make sure the grill has been preheated; the time food takes to cook depends how thick it is and how far it is from the heat source. If the food is thick then lower the tray so it gets a softer heat, which gives it chance to cook through. Any liquid that's on the tray will become extremely hot – so be extra careful when removing the tray. Prime tender meats and fish work best when grilling.

Grilling from below means barbecue time! I am often found in the garden on the barbecue come rain, snow or shine. For one, it eliminates the mess and smoke alarms that are a hazard of grilling indoors, but more than that I love the whole experience of cooking on hot coals. It's really sociable, relaxing and fun, in a way that the kitchen sometimes isn't. Natural heat, great colour and flavour – these are all so brilliant I could easily write a whole book about the joys of the barbecue.

When looking at buying a barbecue you're faced with a massive choice, of which the two main options are gas or charcoal. I have had both over the years and, much as gas is very convenient and instant, I do prefer charcoal. Things to remember:

1. Make sure the barbecue is hot before you start to cook. Get preheating for at least five minutes if it's gas. If you are on coals you will need to wait until the flames have gone and you are left with glowing embers. Don't be tempted to fling your best prime steak onto the orange flames.

2. Marinades deliver exceptional results when barbecued – prepping in advance for the barbecue is always worth the extra effort.

3. Your barbecue is very versatile – much more so than often thought. It can be used for long and slow cookery and the range of food you can cook is endless. Think about the temperatures on the grill, but be brave and experiment. Outdoor cooking really is a joy.

Be bold with meat

Meat tends to be one of the biggest outlays of a weekly shop, but in this book you will find very few recipes that include the prime cuts of meat. We have a saying in the industry that anyone can cook a fillet steak, but it takes skill and understanding to cook the cheaper cuts properly. The cheaper cuts – by which I mean: shins, bellies, shoulders, flanks, ribs and tails – are all working muscles on the animal and because they are hard working, constantly on the move, they become tough. The good news is that all that work develops the most tremendous flavour.

Buying meat can be a minefield – more so than any other ingredient. It's getting easier at the supermarket as the demand for quality local meat is on the up. But even so, if you have a local butcher talk to them about what dish you are looking to create and they will guide you in what to purchase. They will also be happy to provide you with whatever cut you need to your specifications. This helps reduce waste and will help grow your understanding of how to choose, prepare and cook meat – enabling you to be bolder in the dishes you create.

So, search out those cheaper cuts and enjoy the outstanding flavours they provide. But don't forget to be patient and allow the meat the time it needs to cook and rest, too.

Be fearless with fish

It has often puzzled me that we live on a tiny island surrounded by the sea, but as a nation we tend to avoid fish. It's not the easiest thing to buy and loads of people seem to struggle cooking it.

I feel that the days of wrapping a bit of fish in foil and bunging it in the oven are over. Fish is a brilliant thing to cook at home; it's like the ultimate fast food in that it requires very little prep and cooks very quickly. It fits in perfectly with our busy lifestyles. It's also brilliantly healthy and nutritious. Even so, when it comes to filleting your own fish I would always advise not to.

Filleting fish is a skill that takes loads of practice. I would suggest you get the fishmonger to sort out the messy stuff. Sometimes you might have to give it a go especially if you purchase your fish from a supermarket, simply because most supermarket fish counters are serviced by sales staff who are not trained in fish preparation.

Mackerel is the easiest fish to fillet. The flesh comes off very easily, the rib bones can be removed with little effort and the pin bones can be cut out in one go by removing a little flesh along the spine.

If you don't cook much fish, now's your chance

to give it a go. You'll see that all the fishy recipes have everything you need to know in terms of the pitfalls and the best techniques to get glorious results from fish cookery.

Made to last
Batch cooking

Once you have planned and purchased your food, the usual thing to do is fill the fridge and cook when you need to. But I believe times have changed. I love cooking, but the reality is I don't want to come home from work every night and cook. You probably don't either. The answer is to batch cook; it's simpler than you think and saves you loads of time overall.

I cook once a week at home and I love it. I get the music on and lose myself in the kitchen for a few hours. I admit this is much easier in the winter months as the food you want to eat at that time of year lends itself to being stored – curries, stews, pie fillings and soups. On the plus side, if the sun is out you are eating more salads and quick-cook dishes like stir-fries or grills.

Batch cooking drastically cuts your total time in the kitchen per week. You cut prep time because you are doubling up jobs – cutting onions, prepping vegetables, cooking things at the same time. I tend to try and get things off the stove as quickly as I can and finish in a low oven. Depending on your pot size and oven size, you can get a few things in the oven at once – you'll soon find that this saves loads on energy costs.

Once your food is cooked it is vital you look after it properly. If you have made a soup, stew, curry or chilli – fundamentally anything cooked – it must be chilled as quickly as possible. If it's in a pot, pop the pot into an empty sink and top the sink up with cold water until the pot starts to float; you could also pop it in some ice and the food will cool very quickly. If the sink is full, another way to cool the food is to place the pot on top of a wooden spoon. Having the pot at an angle helps circulate the air under the pot and so it cools faster. If food is cooled quickly it will last longer.

Love your leftovers

You have all this food made – now, how best to store it? You have two options, depending on whether it's going in the fridge or freezer. This will come down to how big the batch of food is, and how many people you are going to be feeding.

When it comes to what to store the food in, you have many options. I have used them all.

The first storage solution I used was tubs. I was tub mad – all shapes and sizes filled every cupboard in my kitchen. Tubs are great: easy to use, cheap to buy. The down side is that they take up too much room in fridges and freezers. If you freeze food in a tub it takes ages to defrost, and tub food in the fridge can only be kept for a few days.

Another option is ziplock freezer bags or sandwich bags. Loads of advantages to these: they can be labelled easily, they are cheap to buy and they freeze and defrost quickly as the food is flat in the bag. They take up much less room in the fridge and freezer for the same reason. The food is also protected better, with less chance of freezer burn.

The last option, and the best way to store food, is to vacuum pack it. Yes, vacuum pack it. In the industry we have been using vacuum packers for decades. I was out in a cook shop and spotted a domestic vacuum packer for around £90. Bearing in mind the machines I use in a professional kitchen cost a small fortune, I thought there was little chance that for such a comparatively small outlay this one would do the job. I got it home fully expecting the thing to be back in the box and returned to the shop the following day. To my surprise and amazement the little machine did a brilliant job. Vacuum packing my food at home has saved me loads of cash and I don't think I've thrown away a bit of food since.

Vacuum-packed food has double the 'shelf life' of food kept in a tub – and vacuum packing has all the advantages of zip bags. The downside is the vacuum-pack bags are a little expensive, but you can find them online more cheaply.

How to use this book

Chill out when you cook! It's only a plate of food.

The recipes I have created are detailed, but please don't be put off by the length of a recipe. I have written them in the same way I would describe a lesson, and – like an exam question, but hopefully with more enjoyment – you should always read the whole thing before starting.

When cooking savoury food remember that in most cases you are free to add, substitute, change, add more, or less, of what the recipe states without a kitchen disaster befalling you. If a recipe calls for 400g of mince and your packet is 500g, use the lot. However, the chemistry of baking is more measured. Sweet recipes – and most things made with butter, flour and sugar – need precision.

Butter In my recipes, butter is unsalted; it's much better for working with and I believe it's a better product too. In years gone by, salted butter was cheaper but that's not the case any more.

Oil My recipes call for two different oils. One is 'quality oil' – it's up to you to choose which one. It could be an extra virgin olive oil, or my preference would be a cold pressed rapeseed oil. The flavour is better and it's likely to be local to the area where you purchase it. Cooking oil is exactly what you'd expect: oil for cooking. You can choose from sunflower, vegetable or groundnut.

Eggs These are always large and free range.

Measurements are metric but a conversion chart is included if you need it.

Timing Each recipe indicates cooking time, but not prep time. Prep time is an individual thing depending on how organised or practised you are, if you're cooking with someone else or if you're doing five other jobs at the same time.

Portions Most recipes will make enough to serve four, more or less! Of course, this depends if you're feeding hungry teenagers or not.

THE HASSLE FACTOR

All my recipes serve four and I have created my very own plate rating to indicate the 'hassle factor' for each one.

Ⓖ

1 plate is relatively hassle free.

Ⓖ Ⓖ

2 plates are a wee bit more complex.

Ⓖ Ⓖ Ⓖ

3 plates need planning, time and might be a bit of a challenge.

That said, all the food in *Kitchen Essentials* should be straightforward and enjoyable for anyone who reads the whole recipe and gets organised before they start. It really is all down to planning – once you're organised you can relax and enjoy your cooking!

To joint a chicken

It can be difficult to buy decent quality pre-cut chicken breasts: so, cutting up a chicken is a skill well worth investing in! I'm always disappointed in the vast gulf between what I can buy as a chef and what's available when I go shopping for my family. If you buy a high-welfare chicken, you should get a great product and it's cheaper kilo by kilo to buy the whole bird rather than separate breast meat and legs.

I buy a few whole chickens a week and bone them out. I keep the cuts for different dishes: legs and thighs for long, slow stews and curries, French-trimmed breasts that I keep the skin on and pan roast. The only way to learn to is to give it a go! Even if you cut in the wrong place you can still use the meat and, as always, practice makes perfect.

1. Remove the tips of the wings and the ends of the legs with a large sharp knife. Then remove any string and any remaining feathers.

2. First, spread the legs with a sharp knife, pierce the skin between the leg and the breast.

3. Lift the bird and pull the leg back until the ball and socket and joint pops.

4. Cut the leg off: make sure you get all the meat off the carcass. Do the same on the other side.

5. Next place the chicken onto its back; at the top end of the bird lift the flap of skin and feel for the wishbone. Place a knife into the cavity and scrape down each side of the wishbone. Pull the wishbone out with your fingers.

6. Next remove each breast by carefully cutting down the bone between the breasts until you reach the carcass. Then work the knife around until the breasts have been removed.

7. Trim each breast by removing the chicken wing at the first joint. Now trim the remaining bone and any excess skin.

8. Take each leg and feel where the two bones meet. Cut down sharply to separate the drumstick from the thigh. You should now have 10 pieces of chicken.

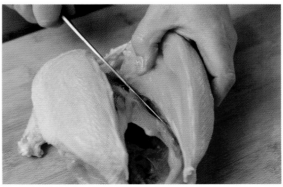

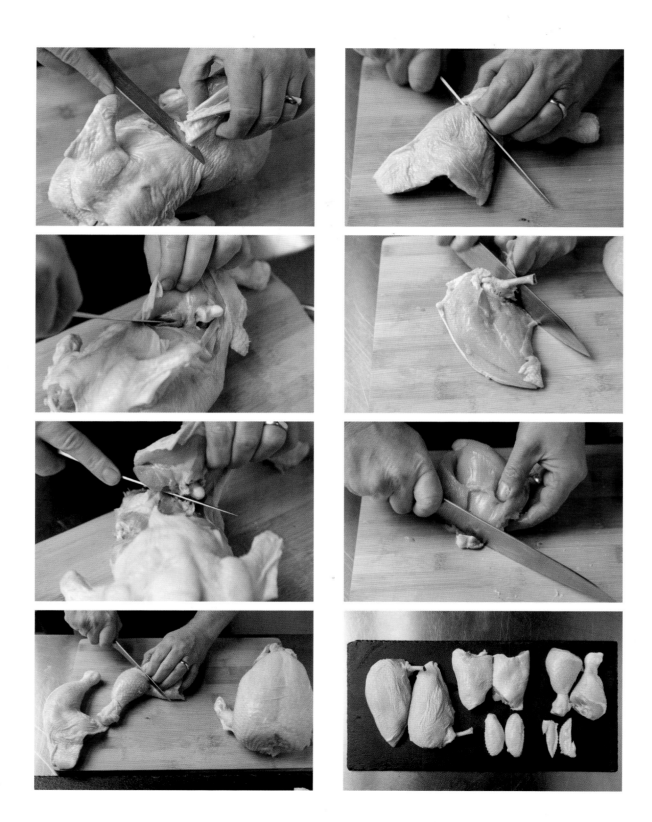

To chop an onion

In my opinion there is nothing more satisfying for a home cook to learn than proper knife skills. And perhaps the most used and most useful knife skill is dicing an onion. Practice makes perfect!

We've all seen TV chefs chopping away superfast and half the time not looking what they're doing. Don't try and copy them! It takes years to develop speed like that. Concentrate on the quality of your technique and the speed will come – eventually.

The first thing to do is make sure your work area is organised. Make sure you are using a good quality chopping board that's safely secured. If your board hasn't got those little rubberised feet to secure it, use a couple of sheets of damp kitchen paper.

Put the board on the work surface about 3 to 4 cm away from the edge. This is to catch anything that falls off the board so it doesn't fall on the floor and end up in the bin. I always like to have a little bowl to put food waste in and a separate bowl to put the onion in once it's chopped.

Now all you need is a good quality sharp knife – see page 7 for knife tips. So, let's get started.

1. The first thing you should always do when cutting vegetables – especially those grown under ground – is wash them before peeling.

2. You are now ready to make the first cut. If you hold up the onion by the stalk the root should be the straggly bit pointing to the ground. Cut off the stalk carefully, making sure you don't cut too far into the onion: you only need to cut about ½ cm from the start of the stalk.

3. Next, peel the onion. I see a lot of home cooks and chefs cut the onion in half at this stage without peeling. This is a bad habit. You need to remove the onion skin before cutting into its flesh; the skin has been in the earth, which is full of fertiliser and you don't really want that all over your chopped onion, do you?

4. Once your onion is peeled give it another wash.

5. Now pop the onion onto the board with the cut side facing the board and cut the onion in half through the root, which should be facing up. The idea is to cut exactly through the root so each half of the onion has equal amounts of root. It's crucial that the root stays on each half, so the onion stays together as you chop it.

6. The next stage is based on you being right handed; if not, swap sides. Take one half of the onion and, on its cut edge, point the root end to the left of the board. Place your left hand on the work surface pointing your fingers straight ahead and, making sure your fingertips don't move, push your hand up into a claw shape.

7. The first knuckle on your middle three fingers that are now exposed are the key to cutting safely and precisely. These three knuckles guide the knife and stop you getting cut. The theory is that if the back third of the blade is in constant contact with those three knuckles you are in control.

8. Using your clawed hand and using your thumb at the back of the onion and your three knuckles at the front, take your cook's knife. Placing the back third of the blade against your knuckles start to draw the knife through the onion using the length of the blade and slicing following the natural lines, moving your three knuckles back a little each time.

9. Try not to chop in a straight downward motion as you won't get full advantage of the shape of the knife; instead pull back through the onion. Also try not to cut all the way through the back of the onion as it will fall to bits. Cut the lines of the onion all the way to the end.

10. Next, adjust your claw hand so your knuckles are pointing towards the right of the board and, using your thumb and pinkie finger, hold the onion together and, once again using your three knuckles as a guide for the knife, start cutting through your earlier cuts.

11. Super fine chopped onion will now appear with each slice of the knife.

12. If you have an end bit left lie it flat and chop it in the same way as you would chopped herbs.

Pastry skills

For some of my recipes, you need to line a mould or ring with pastry, and then bake that pastry blind. This is easy if you follow some simple rules.

To line a ring with pastry

1. To create a successful pastry tart you need decent pastry. Overworked pastry is difficult to manage and will shrink a lot when cooked.

2. My recipes ask that you rest the pastry, and also that you flatten it before you rest it. This helps stop shrinkage. Resting the pastry flat means you can pin it straight from the fridge.

3. Take your time when rolling pastry and don't use too much flour on the surface, as this can dry the pastry out. When rolling, only push the rolling pin backwards and forwards: you should turn the pasty and not the pin.

4. If you turn the pastry each time you pin it, you will get a much more even pastry. As you're moving the pastry at every turn, you can also guarantee that it isn't sticking to the surface.

5. To line a large case, mould or ring, use the rolling pin to pick the pastry up. This stops the pastry splitting or breaking when you lift it. Do this by placing the rolling pin at one end of the pastry and rolling the pastry around the pin.

6. Carefully roll the pastry over the ring. Next cohere the pastry into the shape of the ring.

7. Now take a bit of spare pastry and use it to push the pastry into the corner and flutes of the ring. You will now have a pastry overhang around the ring, which gives you two options.

8. The first is to take it off. To do this, roll the pin right over the top of the ring so as to cut off any excess pastry. Then use your fingers to push the cut edge up and over the flan ring. This provides a little room for shrinkage. I only ever cut the pastry when I know it's perfect.

10. The second is to bake the pastry with the overhang. This always gives you a finish that is nice and neat to the top of the ring.

11. If you have lots of individual rings or moulds to line, roll out all the pastry until it's a bit thicker than you need. Then take a plain scone cutter a little bigger than the rings you're lining and cut out as many as you can from the pastry.

12. Roll out each pastry circle a little more thinly before using it to line each individual ring.

To bake blind

Baking blind is the process of cooking the pastry before the filling goes in. You do this to ensure the pastry is nice and crisp.

1. Once rolled, place your lined rings in the fridge to rest and harden up for at least 30 minutes.

2. Next take your pastry-lined ring and cover it with three sheets of cling film.

3. Now fill the ring with baking beans. You can buy these little ceramic or metal balls from cook shops. Or you can use dried pulses or rice.

4. When the case is filled, bring the excess cling film up and over and scrunch it together to form a pouch. I know: *cling film in the oven?* Yes, I promise it works. As long as you have three layers it won't burst.

6. Now place in the oven at 180°C and bake until the pastry edges start to colour.

7. Remove from the oven and let it settle for a few minutes.

8. Take the cling film parcels off from the pastry. The bottom of the pastry still needs more cooking, but first take an egg, break it into a bowl and brush the pastry with it, making sure the egg covers all the pastry. This provides a waterproof barrier, which ensures the pastry stays crisp once you have put in your filling.

9. Pop the pastry back into the oven and bake until evenly cooked.

10 Allow the pastry to cool before removing any overhang. You are now ready to use the pastry cases.

GETTING STARTED

When I sat down to write this book I had no plans to do a section on starters. But I found that as I was writing, some dishes popped up that can only be described as starters. I know that unless you are hosting a posh dinner party the reality is that you are not making starters for a Tuesday night tea. Which means that the dishes I have included in this chapter are perfect for loads of different occasions when a starter or small bite-style food could work. Parties, Christmas and other celebration lunches, special dinners or those times that you want something a little lighter. I have included one recipe in this chapter that is a variant on a dish I created on MasterChef.

2

1. **Goats cheese** with salt pickled beetroot, chutney and toasted hazelnuts

For the beetroot

1 candy stripe or golden beetroot

50g sugar

50ml white wine vinegar

1 clove

1 star anise

1 sprig of thyme

For the oatcakes

100g plain flour, sifted

Pinch of salt

Pinch bicarbonate of soda

440g porridge oats

100g butter

320ml boiling water

For the chutney

200g beetroot

1 braeburn apple

1 banana shallots

50g soft brown sugar

30ml white wine vinegar

1 orange, zested and juiced

1/2 tsp ground ginger

1/2 tsp coriander seeds

1/2 cinnamon stick

Pinch of cumin

Pinch of cayenne pepper

For the goats cheese

1 soft goats cheese, I like to use Glazert as it's local to me.

75g hazelnuts

10g chives

50g gingerbread, optional

Micro red chard, to garnish

This is quite a simple dish, but it relies on great ingredients and precise cooking to make it amazing.

Pickled beetroot

1. Put all ingredients except the beetroot in a pot and bring up to boil. Then take off from the heat.
2. Meanwhile, using a mandolin or a very sharp knife, cut the beetroot into very thin slices.
3. Place the slices into the hot pickling liquor and leave them in the pot until needed and the liquor has cooled.

Oatcakes

1. Mix oats (save a handful for rolling), salt, bicarb of soda and flour.
2. Melt the butter in a jug of boiling water and add to the dry ingredients.
3. Mix with your hands until the mixture feels spongy.
4. Sprinkle some oats on to your work surface, then turn the mixture out and scatter more oats on top.
5. Pin out with a rolling pin until the mix is about 5 mm thick, then cut to required shape.
6. Bake on a greased baking tray at 180°C for 10 minutes.

Beetroot chutney

1. Finely dice the beetroot, then grate the apple keeping the skin on.
2. Place in a pot with all the other ingredients.
3. Bring up to the boil then turn down to a gentle simmer.
4. Cook out slowly for about 35 minutes or until the majority of the liquid has gone.
5. You should be left with nice sticky chutney.

Goats cheese

1. Place the goats cheese into a food processor for a few seconds and then roll up into a log shape.
2. Place the goats cheese on to a sheet of cling film with a sprinkle of chives and hazelnuts, and crumbed gingerbread.
3. Roll up together and put into the fridge.

To serve

1. When you're ready, arrange everything on platters, garnish with the red chard and help yourself.

2. Cantaloupe melon with summer berries

1 cantaloupe melon

200g mixed summer berries

This simple dish is best prepared when the berries are in season.

1. Your first job is to prepare the melon. First cut the top and the bottom off the melon. This will provide a flat edge for the melon to stand up safely.

2. Next, using a carving knife, cut a thin strip of skin from the melon from the top cut edge all the way down to the bottom cut edge. This should reveal the bright orange flesh of the melon. Do this all the way around the melon until all the skin has been removed. Please try and follow the shape of the melon so that by the end of the peeling process the melon is still round.

3. Halve the peeled melon and remove the seeds. Next cut the thinnest wedges you can from each half. Now trim the wedges so that the curved edge is on the inside of the straight.

4. To create the fan star shape, I use two pastry cutters – one small and one large. Place the large cutter in the centre of the plate, then place your thinly cut melon around the cutter one on top of the other until you reach all the way around. Tuck the last slice of melon under the first one you put down.

5. Remove the large ring and place the small ring in the centre of the plate. Now carefully push the slices of melon while keeping them all together towards the small ring. This will magically produce the star shape.

6. Fill the space that is left with your summer berries.

3. Tomato lettuce cups with feta and pomegranate

1 red pepper, or small bell pepper, sliced small

1 medium red onion, peeled and finely diced

1 head cos lettuce

2 medium tomatoes, firm, ripe and on the vine

200g feta cheese

1 pomegranate, deseeded

2 sprigs of mint, shredded

Handful of oregano, shredded

Handful of flat parsley, shredded

3 tbs quality oil

Sea salt, if required

This dish has sweet and salty with the pomegranate and the feta, it has lots of freshness from the herbs and the tomato. The combination works very well as a palate refresher.

1. Top and tail, halve, core, deseed and thinly slice the pepper.
2. Place in a large bowl with the onion and the pomegranate seeds.
3. Halve and deseed the tomatoes, then cut into small cubes or thin slices and add to the bowl.
4. Dice the feta and add to the salad with the parsley. Drizzle over the olive oil and toss the salad carefully.
5. Prepare the lettuce so that you can use the bigger leaves as a 'cup' to hold the salad.
6. Taste for seasoning – some feta is quite salty. Transfer your salad to the lettuce cups and scatter over the mint and oregano.

4. Pan seared scallops with black pudding, carrot purée, crispy shallots and onion seeds

12 king scallops
12 slices of black pudding
300g carrots
50g butter
2 banana shallots
50g plain flour
1/2 lemon, juiced
Few sprigs of dill
Cooking oil
Onion seeds to finish

This is quite a simple dish, but it relies on great ingredients and precise cooking to make it stand out. A lot of people are a bit put off by black pudding, but don't be – it's a brilliant, tasty ingredient.

1. Your first task is to make the carrot purée. To do this you need to peel, wash and chop the carrots into even-sized pieces.

2. Place the carrots into a pot with half of the butter and a little salt. Cover with water and bring to the boil.

3. Once the carrots have cooked drain them into a colander over a bowl to catch the cooking liquor.

4. Pour the carrots into your liquidiser and blitz down. You might have to add some of the cooking liquor to get it going, but be careful not to add too much as it will make it too watery.

5. Adjust the seasoning and put to one side.

6. Next take your black pudding and evenly slice it. I use baby black pudding so the slices are smaller. You can use what is local to you – visit your butcher.

7. Next cut your shallots into thin rings and dust with flour. Then in a small pan with a little oil shallow fry until crisp and put to one side.

8. Next pop your black pudding on a baking tray into a moderate oven – around 170°C. (It will take between 10 and 15 minutes to cook.)

9. Now it's time to cook your scallops. Place your pan on the heat and once it's hot add a little oil.

10. Place the scallops into the pan in a clockwise direction starting at 12 o'clock, 1 o'clock and so on. The reason for this is so you know exactly what order the scallops went in the pan so you will know the order in which to remove them.

11. Once your first scallop has taken on some colour it's ready to turn.

12. Quickly turn all your scallops, and once they have all been turned remove the pan from the heat, squeeze in some fresh lemon juice and the remainder of the butter.

13. Coat all the scallops with the lemon and butter mixture and remove from the pan. Place the scallops on some kitchen paper to absorb any excess butter.

14. By this time your black pudding should be cooked. Now arrange the pudding on the plate topped with the scallops and crispy shallots.

15. Add your carrot purée and finish with a few sprigs of dill and onion seeds.

5. **Black pudding** with diced garlic potatoes and fried egg

1 black pudding, sliced and diced

500g potatoes good for frying, diced

2 cloves of garlic, crushed

4 eggs

Cooking oil

Bunch of flat parsley, shredded

Sprig of thyme

This is a very easy dish to make and is perfect for a lazy, nourishing Sunday brunch.

1. Preheat your oven to 200°C.
2. The first thing you need to do is to dice the potatoes and place them into a frying pan with a little oil and fry until golden and crisp.
3. Add the black pudding and cook until the pudding starts to crisp up, then add the crushed garlic and picked thyme, cook out for a couple of minutes.
4. The last thing to add is the shredded flat parsley.
5. Split this mixture into four ovenproof dishes, and put in the oven to keep warm.
6. Lastly fry the egg. You could crack the egg and place directly onto a baking tray in the oven, or like I have done shallow fry the egg.
7. To do this you will need a frying pan with about ½ cm of oil in it. The secret of success when frying eggs is to not have the pan too hot when the egg goes into the oil – it shouldn't make any sound. Using your spatula flick the oil over the top of the egg controlling the temperature as you go.
8. Your aim when cooking a fried egg is to keep the yolk runny.
9. Slide an egg onto each of your pots and serve.

6. Smoked duck breast with fig, walnut and orange salad

2 smoked duck breasts
1 orange, segmented
2 sticks celery
4 fresh figs
1 red onion, finely sliced
1 salad cress
100g walnuts

For the dressing

1 red chilli, finely diced
1/2 lemon, juiced and zested
100ml quality oil
Salt and pepper, to season

This dish looks stunning and makes use of fresh figs, which are sumptuous but can be tricky to buy at that 'just right' moment. Look out for Turkish and Mediterranean figs, and also the new crops of figs grown in the south of England.

1. Slice the duck breast as thin as you can and put to one side.

2. To segment the orange, top and tail the orange, then place the orange on one of the cut ends and using your knife cut thin strips of peel from top to bottom all the way around the orange until all the peel has been removed.

3. To remove the flesh from the orange, carefully cut between the pith and the flesh on each side and the segments will just fall away.

4. Peel and slice the celery into thin strips and place into ice water to crisp up.

5. Cut the figs into quarters, or smaller slices as you wish.

6. Assemble all the ingredients onto the plate as you see fit. You can build your salad up in layers or even mix all the ingredients together.

7. To make the dressing, finely dice the chilli, zest and juice the lemon, and mix with the oil. Season to taste.

8. Finish your salad with the dressing.

7. Potted Arbroath smokie with oatcakes

For the potted smokie

2 Arbroath smokies

280g cream cheese

100g crème fraîche

30g wholegrain mustard

1 bunch of chives, finely chopped

1 banana shallot, chopped

50g butter

2 sprigs of thyme

Seasoning

For the oatcakes

100g plain flour, sifted

Pinch of salt

Pinch bicarbonate of soda

440g porridge oats

100g butter

320ml boiling water

This is a simple dish to make and the flavour from the smokies is amazing. If you can't get smokies you can always replace them with smoked mackerel fillets.

The oatcakes recipe is one I used on *MasterChef* on the 'Chef's Table' episode. I decided to create a hoop with the mix. The only thing that drove me mad from the show is that the commentator called it an oat tuile. An oat tuile is easy but an oatcake hoop is much more technical and difficult. You can cut it any way you wish, but if you are brave you can try the hoop. Good luck!

1. To start you need to prepare the fish. Start by opening the fish up and carefully remove the back bone and the ribs, these bones should come away easily and this should separate the two fillets.

2. Run your fingers along the flesh to feel for stray bones, and remove them if you find any. Next peel away the skin.

3. Place the fish into a bowl, add the chopped shallot, mustard, chopped chives, crème fraîche and the cream cheese.

4. Add a few twists of black pepper, then with a wooden spoon start to mix all the ingredients together.

5. I like a bit of texture so I tend not to mix it too much. Once mixed, double check the seasoning and when you are happy with it split the mix between your serving dishes.

6. Next take your butter and clarify. To do this melt the butter in a pot and carefully boil until the buttermilk has evaporated and all you are left with is the oil.

7. Allow the butter to cool slightly, pick the leaves from the thyme and pop into the warm butter for the flavour to infuse.

8. Make sure the potted smokie is flat as can be, then spoon the clarified thyme butter over the pate to create a thin layer over the top.

9. Set in the fridge until needed.

Oatcakes

1. See recipe 1 on page 25 for how to make oatcakes.

8. Steamed mussels

This recipe is inspired by a day I spent harvesting mussels in Shetland. They were so good that I decided to steam them rather than anything more fancy – the result was the best thing I've tasted in my life. Everyone has a different method for this iconic dish, here's mine – it involves cooking them very, very quickly.

2kg mussels, fresh

50g butter

2 shallots, finely diced

200ml white wine

1/2 bunch of flat leaf parsley, chopped

Lemons, cut into wedges to garnish

A squeeze of lemon

Salt and pepper, to taste

1. You will need a large pan with a tight-fitting lid. You might have to cook the mussels in batches depending on the size of your pan.

2. The first job is to clean the mussels. Wash them under cold running water, using a table knife to scrape away any barnacles. You also have to remove any beards by pulling out the beards that protrude from between the closed shells.

3. If you find any mussels are open, then give then a short little tap on the side of the sink. This should encourage them to close. If they don't close they should be thrown away as they are most likely dead.

4. Now place the cleaned mussels into a bowl and add the chopped shallots, butter, salt, pepper and wine.

5. Place your pan onto the heat and heat it up as hot as you can without burning the pot.

6. Once the pot is hot pour in the mussels with the rest of the ingredients and – quick as you can – put the lid on.

7. The idea is that the heat from the pan creates instant steam, which cooks the mussels very quickly.

8. Don't look in the pot! You will lose the steam and stop the cooking. Another thing to avoid is shaking the pan. If you shake the pot the mussels will fall out of the shell and you'll be left with a bowl of empty shells.

9. After a few minutes, if you have managed to keep the steam in, the mussels should be cooked. Have a little look and if the mussels are wide open they are ready.

10. Spoon the mussels into your serving bowls, discarding any that have not opened.

11. To finish sprinkle with chopped parsley, a squeeze of lemon juice and a couple of lemon wedges.

Don't kill your mussels!

When storing mussels keep them in the little net on a tray covered with a damp tea towel in the fridge until you are ready to prepare them. Do not be tempted to store them in water. If you have them stored for any length of time it's a good idea to refresh them under running water just for a couple of minutes and this will help keep them longer and also clean them out.

9. **Spring rolls** with goats cheese and red pepper

200g goats cheese
1 red pepper
1 red chilli
1 red onion
1/2 bunch of coriander, shredded
1/2 tsp of paprika
2 tsp vegetable oil
12 spring roll wrappers
1 egg, to glue wrappers

There's a stir-fry element to this recipe, which means my top tip is – don't stir your stir-fry!

1. The first task is to prepare all the vegetables. Top and tail the pepper and then cut it in half. Remove the pith and the seeds. Lay the pepper flat on the chopping board and slice thinly, then do the same with the other half and the ends.

2. Cut the chilli in half, then deseed and dice it. Peel and slice the red onion. Now shred the coriander.

3. Next in a large frying pan or wok, stir-fry the pepper, onion and chilli. Once the vegetables have softened remove from the heat to cool.

4. While the mix is cooling break the goats cheese up into 1 cm chunks. And once it's cool, add the shredded coriander and the cheese.

5. Sprinkle with paprika and give the lot a good mix.

6. Taste and adjust the seasoning.

7. Preheat your oven to 200°C.

8. Working with one wrapper at a time (cover remaining wrappers to prevent drying), place the wrapper in front of you in a diamond shape, spoon a little of the cheese vegetable mixture into the front and centre of the wrapper.

9. Fold the bottom point of the wrapper over the mixture and pull it tight to create a tight roll.

10. Brush the left and right corners with beaten egg.

11. Fold the right corner over the vegetable mixture, then fold the lower left over.

12. Moisten the top corner with beaten egg.

13. Roll up as tight as you can to create your spring roll.

14. Repeat until all your mixture has been used up. By the end of the mix you will be an expert.

15. Coat your spring rolls with a little oil and place them on a baking tray.

16. Bake at 200°C for 18 minutes or until golden brown, turning the spring rolls over halfway through.

10. Arancini with spicy Italian sausage stuffed with pine nuts and mozzarella

2 Italian sausages

120g Arborio rice

2 shallots, finely diced

2 clove of garlic, finely minced

2 red chilli, finely diced

2 tbsp flat parsley, chopped

50g butter

Pinch of salt

600ml chicken stock, a quality stock cube will work for this

50g Parmesan, grated

100ml white wine

50g pine nuts, toasted

1 ball of mozzarella

Cooking oil

For the crumb mix

200g panko breadcrumbs

100g plain flour, seasoned

Pinch of paprika

2 eggs, lightly beaten

50ml milk

These stuffed rice balls are made with panko breadcrumbs, which are super crunchy.

1. The first thing to do is make the risotto. Heat some oil and 25g of the butter in a large pan over a medium heat. Add the chopped shallot and cook for about 2 minutes, stirring, until soft and translucent.

2. Stir in the rice and cook for a further 2 minutes. The rice should start to crackle.

3. Remove the skin from the sausage and break it up into the hot rice and cook until the sausage has all been coloured.

4. Turn up the heat and add the white wine – it should sizzle as it hits the pan. Cook for about 2 minutes to evaporate the alcohol.

5. Add the crushed garlic and chopped chilli. Adding the garlic at a later stage in the cooking ensures the garlic doesn't burn and ruin the dish.

6. Once the liquid has reduced, begin adding the hot stock a ladleful at a time over a medium heat, allowing each addition to be absorbed before adding the next, and stirring continuously.

7. The rice should always be moist but not swimming in liquid. The process of adding and stirring should take between 15 and 20 minutes.

8. Once the rice is cooked add the grated Parmesan cheese, chopped parsley and the toasted pine nuts. You can toast pine nuts by putting them in a dry frying pan over a medium heat for 3 minutes. Keep shoogling the pan so they don't burn.

9. Double check for seasoning and spread the rice out on a flat tray and allow to cool.

10. Take your mozzarella ball and cut into ½ cm cubes.

11. Once the rice mixture is cool, take a heaped tablespoonful of it, place a cube of mozzarella in the centre, then roll it between your palms to form a ball about 4 to 5 cm in diameter. Set aside on a plate while you roll the rest of the rice mixture.

12. Put the flour in a dish and mix in the paprika and some seasoning. Mix the eggs with the milk, then put the breadcrumbs and the egg mix in two more separate dishes.

13. Take a rice ball and roll first in the flour, then in the egg, and finally in the breadcrumbs. Shake off any excess crumbs and set aside on a clean plate. Repeat with the remaining rice balls.

14. Preheat a deep-fat fryer or pan of oil to 180°C. Gently lower the rice balls into the pan in batches and cook for 3 to 4 minutes, or until golden brown. Remove with a slotted or wire spoon and drain on kitchen paper.

15. Serve immediately.

11. Spiced confit duck summer rolls with pickled cabbage, ginger and lime

2 duck legs

1 orange, zested

30g sea salt

500ml duck fat

1/2 red onion

1/2 red chilli

1/2 carrot

15g ginger, peeled and diced

Handful of bean sprouts

1/8 Chinese cabbage

30ml rice wine vinegar

20g honey

1 lemon grass, bashed

20g toasted sesame seeds

8 sheets rice paper, can be bought in any good oriental supermarket

2 tbsp soy sauce, for dipping

These gorgeous little delicacies are a real treat. Once you have mastered the technique of filling the rice paper wrapper with heaps of fresh flavours then you can experiment with ingredients – to create delicious bite-size parcels of contrasting tastes and textures. I use duck in this recipe, which you will need to prepare the day before.

1. The first thing to do is prepare the confit duck legs.
2. Take the sea salt and rub this into the duck legs, zest the orange and rub that into the legs. Put the legs into a bag and place in the fridge overnight. This will cure the meat and help keep the duck pink even after three hours of cooking.
3. The following day wash off the salt and orange zest.
4. Place the duck into an ovenproof dish and cover with the duck fat. Cook in a low oven at 130°C for three hours until the meat is tender. Once cooled, pick the meat from the bone and put to one side.
5. The next job is to make the pickle for the cabbage. Put the vinegar and diced ginger, honey and bashed lemon grass in a small pot. Bring the vinegar to the boil, remove from the heat and taste for balance.
6. Shred the cabbage into a bowl then pour over the pickling liquor.
7. Cut the chilli, carrot and onion into fine matchsticks and mix together with the bean sprouts.
8. Soak the rice papers one at a time in a large bowl of ice cold water. Once the papers are soft carefully remove and pat dry with kitchen paper.
9. Lay the rice paper sheets out onto your work surface and start to build the layers of the roll.
10. First, sprinkle the toasted sesame seeds onto the paper then the duck leg and next the pickled cabbage. Last of all are the matchstick vegetables.
11. Carefully fold the rice paper over and cover the mix with the paper then pull back, making sure you have a tight round cylinder. Tuck in the edges and finish off rolling.
12. This can be served whole or cut into three pieces for easy dipping.

12. Crispy Korean chicken wings with kimchi cabbage

1kg chicken wings

75ml soy sauce

100g Korean chilli paste (Gochujang)

1 tbsp red chilli flakes

1 tbsp rice vinegar

75g honey

50g ginger, minced

50g garlic, minced

150g cornflour

75g sesame seeds

Oil for deep-frying

For the kimchi cabbage

500g Chinese cabbage

30g coarse sea salt

25g chilli flakes

1 tbsp sugar

20g fish sauce

4 cloves of garlic, minced

5 stalks of spring onion, chopped

2 large carrots, cut into fine matchsticks

For maximum flavour, marinate these delicious chicken wings for as long as possible. If you can prepare a day in advance then do so – they'll taste all the better for it. And don't worry about what you'll do with any leftover chilli paste – these wings are so good you'll make them again and again.

1. First, make the marinade. Mix the soy sauce, chilli paste, chilli flakes, rice vinegar, honey, ginger and garlic in a bowl.

2. Place your chicken wings into large ziploc bag. The preparation of the wings is up to you. Some people prefer them to be served whole or cut into joints.

3. Pour the mixed ingredients into the bag with the wings. Push out all the air in the bag and zip it shut. Carefully massage the mix into the chicken wings.

4. Place the bag into the fridge for as long as possible – 24 hours would be brilliant.

5. When you are ready to cook the chicken, remove the wings from the bag. The trick is not to have too much sauce on the wings, but in saying that you still need some sauce … but not too much!

6. Mix the sesame seeds and the cornflour together. Next – a few wings at a time – coat them with the sesame seeds and the cornflour.

7. Now preheat your wok with oil. Be careful at this stage; the purpose of deep-frying is to instantly crisp up the chicken.

8. Deep-fry the chicken in small batches until all the chicken is crispy.

9. Next place the chicken into a preheated oven at 200°C until the chicken is fully cooked.

Kimchi cabbage

1. This is an easy version of making kimchi: you can make and serve it all in the same day.

2. Cut the cabbage into thin strips 2 cm wide, place into a large bowl, add 200ml of cold water and the coarse sea salt. Mix the salt in with your hands and set to one side for 15 minutes.

3. Mix the remaining ingredients together to make a hot paste.

4. Wash and rinse the salted cabbage in cold water a couple of times then drain the water.

5. Thoroughly mix the kimchi paste into the cabbage.

6. Put the kimchi into a container, jar or plastic bag, ensuring all the air has been removed.

7. Eat it right away, or keep it at room temperature for a few days and it will ferment.

13. Vegetable pakora and raita

300g chickpea flour
(gram flour)

1 cauliflower, finely
chopped

1 courgette, finely diced

1 red onion, finely diced

1/2 pack of baby spinach,
shredded

1/2 bunch of coriander
leaves, shredded

1 green chilli, finely diced

1 tsp chilli powder

1 tsp ground cumin

1/2 tsp ground coriander

1 tsp tandoori masala
powder

500ml of vegetable oil,
for deep-frying

Salt and pepper

For the raita

1 cucumber, peeled if you
prefer

1/2 bunch of mint, picked
and shredded

300g natural yogurt

1/2 tsp garam masala

To serve

A few slices of red onion

Garam masala, to dust

Practice really does make perfect with these delicious snacks. I always do a little test batch to make sure I have the seasoning correct. And the raita makes the perfect, refreshing dip for your pakora.

1. Place all the prepared vegetables and herbs into a large bowl.
2. Add all the spices, salt and pepper.
3. Next add about 200ml of cold water to the bowl.
4. With your hands start mixing the water, vegetables and spices and then gradually start adding the chickpea or gram flour.
5. You are trying to achieve a consistency that is sticky and moist. It is not like a batter – it's much more like a paste.
6. To cook the pakora you will need your oil to be about 165°C. This is a slower style of deep-frying as you need to cook out the vegetables and the flour.
7. To cook you will need a little bowl of water nearby. Wet your hands and then take a golf ball amount of mix and flatten it out and carefully place into the hot oil.
8. Do this until all the mix has been through the oil.
9. You can pre-make the pakoras and simply warm them through in a hot oven when you need them.
10. When ready to serve top with a little sliced red onion and a dusting of garam masala.

For the raita
1. Finely dice the cucumber; try and remove the centre seeds.
2. Add the shredded mint leaves, then mix in the yogurt.
3. Check the seasoning and finish with the garam masala.

14. Onion bhaji

1 red onion, finely sliced

1 white onion, finely sliced

1 green chilli, finely chopped

2 cloves of garlic

3 cm of root ginger, finely diced or grated

1/2 tsp red chilli powder

1/2 tsp ground turmeric

1/4 tsp cumin seeds, dry roasted in a hot pan

200g gram flour

3 tbsp rice flour

1/4 bunch of coriander, chopped

500ml of vegetable oil, for deep-frying

Garam masala, for dusting

Salt and pepper

This is a very similar process to the pakora – it's lovely to make them at the same time and serve with raita as a dip. As with the pakora, it's good to do a test batch to make sure you have the seasoning correct.

1. Place the onions, garlic, chilli, coriander and ginger into a large bowl.
2. Add all the spices, salt and pepper.
3. Next add about 100ml of cold water to the bowl.
4. With your hands, start mixing the water, onions and spices together.
5. Now gradually start adding the gram flour and the rice flour.
6. You are trying to achieve a consistency that is sticky and moist. It is not like a batter – it's much more like a paste.
7. To cook the bhajis you will need your oil to be about 165°C. This slower style of deep-frying cooks the vegetables and the flour.
8. To cook you will need a little bowl of water nearby. Wet your hands and then take a golf ball amount of mix and flatten it out and carefully place into the hot oil. I prefer to flatten the mix as it gives you a more crispy surface area and less stodge in the middle.
9. Do this until all the mix has been through the oil.
10. You can pre-make the bhajis and simply heat them through a hot oven when you need them.
11. When ready to serve top with a dusting of garam masala.

15. Spiced onions

2 large onions, sliced super thin

1 tsp chilli powder

1/2 tsp ground cumin

150g tomato ketchup

1/2 bunch of coriander, shredded

1/2 bunch of mint, shredded

2 tbsp of mango chutney

Salt and pepper

This is a super simple recipe with some great flavours that takes no time at all to prepare.

1. The first thing is to put the sliced onions into a large bowl, then season with salt and pepper.
2. Next dust with chilli powder and ground cumin.
3. Add the shredded herbs, ketchup and mango chutney.
4. Double check the seasoning and serve.

16. Paneer with butternut squash, spicy onion, chilli and squash crisps

1 butternut squash

200g paneer cheese, diced

100g yogurt

1/2 tsp tumeric

1/2 tsp chilli

1/2 tsp cumin

1/2 white onion, sliced

1 red chilli

50g chilli sauce

Small bunch of coriander, shredded

Cooking oil

The taste of this is wonderful – especially if you leave it to marinate overnight so the flavours can develop.

1. The first job is to mix the spices with the yogurt, then add the diced paneer cheese. Leave to marinate – overnight if possible.

2. To prepare the butternut squash, cut the top and the bottom off the squash, then cut it in half.

3. Place the squash on its flattest surface, then peel the skin off a little strip at a time working around the squash until the skin has been removed.

4. To remove the seeds from the bottom half of the squash you need to halve the squash from top to bottom and take them out. The seeds can be roasted in a little olive oil and sea salt if you wish.

5. Cut the butternut squash into dice, saving some to make the squash crisps later.

6. Slice the onion and place in a warm pan with a little oil. Then slowly cook until the onion is soft and has taken on a little colour.

7. Next add the chopped chilli and the chilli sauce, and put to one side.

8. To bring the dish together place the diced butternut squash in a hot pan with a little oil. Once the squash is soft add the paneer with the yogurt marinade and cook until the yogurt has coated the cheese and the squash.

9. Put the chilli and onion into a dish, then top with the paneer and squash mix.

10. Using some of the squash, peel long strips and dust in flour. Then place the strips into a deep fryer at about 160°C. This will give you some very crunchy butternut squash to create a real contrast in texture.

11. Place the squash crisps on top of the dish, garnish with coriander and serve.

17. Cullen skink

1 large potato, peeled and
   cut into 1 cm cubes

25g butter

1 onion, finely diced, or a
   leek if you feel brave

125g pale smoked
   haddock fillet

1 bay leaf

375ml milk

25ml double cream

Salt and pepper

The cullen skink is a true king of soups. I once got into hot water when I put leeks and a poached egg in a video of how to make it. I learned fast that the people of the northeast don't like their traditional Scottish recipes messed with.

1. Melt a knob of butter in a saucepan big enough to accommodate the fish.

2. Cook the onion on a medium heat for a few minutes without colouring, until soft.

3. Sit the smoked haddock in a fresh pan along with the bay leaf. Pour in some of the milk, just topping the fish.

4. Bring to a simmer and cook for 4 to 6 minutes, depending on the thickness of the fish.

5. Remove the fish from the pan and keep to one side.

6. Add the chopped potato, onion and the remaining milk to your pan. Leave to cook for 15 to 20 minutes, until the potato is tender.

7. While this is cooking, remove the skin and any bones from the haddock, and flake.

8. When the soup is ready, remove the bay leaf.

9. Add the double cream and season with salt and pepper.

10. Add the flaked haddock and bring back to a warm temperature ready to serve.

18. Pea and ham soup

300g peas, frozen are
  perfect

1 carrot

1 onion

1/2 leek

2 sticks of celery

4 cloves of garlic, crushed

1.5 litres of ham stock, a
  good quality cube works
  for this

2 bay leaves

6 slices of cured ham

2 spring onions, chopped

20g quality oil

Seasoning

With its distinctive colour and flavour combinations, this is an absolute classic of a soup.

1. Your first job is to prepare the vegetables. Wash and peel all the vegetables, then finely chop the onion, celery, leek and carrot. Don't worry too much about the size as it's going to get blended.

2. In a large, thick-bottomed pan add the oil. Once you have a little heat, add the chopped vegetables. Cook down the vegetables without achieving colour. We are trying to extract as much flavour as we can from the vegetables as this is going to form the base of the soup.

3. Once the vegetables are soft put in half the cured ham and the garlic, mix in with the vegetables.

4. Next add the stock and the bay leaves, and bring to the boil.

5. The last thing is to add is the frozen peas. Once you've added the peas bring the soup to the boil, then blend until smooth.

6. To finish top with some chopped spring onion and shredded cured ham.

19. Spicy red lentil soup

175g split red lentils, washed

1 onion, chopped

2 celery sticks, peeled and chopped

1 carrot, peeled and chopped

1 garlic clove, crushed

1 tsp ground cumin

1/2 tsp ground coriander

1/2 tsp red chilli flakes

1.5 litres of vegetable stock, a good quality cube works well

4 tsp tomato purée

1 tbsp quality oil

1 bay leaf

2 spring onions, shredded to serve

This is a delicious, filling soup. It's ideal for coming home to on a cold evening. The mix of flavours from the spices makes it even more warming and satisfying.

1. Heat the oil in a pan.
2. Add the chopped onion and cook over a low heat for 5 to 6 minutes, until beginning to soften.
3. Stir in the celery and carrot and cook for 2 minutes.
4. Add the garlic, chilli flakes, cumin and coriander and cook for a further minute.
5. Add the washed lentils, stock, tomato purée and bay leaf.
6. Bring to the boil, reduce the heat, then cover the pan with a lid and simmer for 20 to 25 minutes until the lentils and vegetables are very soft.
7. Remove the bay leaf from the soup.
8. Blend the soup in the pan using a hand-held blender; or tip into a food processor, process until smooth, then return the soup to the pan.
9. Check the consistency; it will be fairly thick, so if you prefer it thinner, add a little more stock.
10. Season to taste, top with a little oil and shredded spring onions.

20. Cannellini bean and pancetta soup

150g smoked pancetta, diced

2 tins of cannellini beans, drained and rinsed

1 stick celery, peeled and finely diced

1 small onion, finely diced

1 clove garlic, crushed

1/2 carrot, finely diced

150ml stock, you could use a quality cube

20g butter

1 tsp cooking oil

Salt and pepper

This is a delicious thick soup, very quick to make. If you don't have cannellini beans you can use butter beans or black-eye beans . . . just remember to rinse them well.

1. Heat a sauté pan and add a teaspoon of oil.

2. When the pan is nice and hot add the diced pancetta and cook for 3 to 4 minutes or until golden brown.

3. Now add all the vegetables, garlic and butter and sweat for 3 to 4 minutes.

4. Add one tin of the beans and pour in stock, then bring to the boil.

5. Once boiling, turn down to a simmer and cook for 10 to 15 minutes. Once all the vegetables are tender, the soup is ready to be liquidised. A hand-held blender will do the job nicely.

6. Once the soup is smooth, add the remaining tin of beans and bring back to the boil.

7. Check the seasoning, then serve with a doorstop of bread and butter.

WHAT'S FOR SUPPER?

Well, what is for supper? We have all done it – we've come home and there's nothing prepared and the fridge is empty. Which means that this section is perfect for when you aren't exactly organised but still want real food for dinner. Here you will find very quick and easy recipes that you can do from scratch without much prep time. One pot or pan stuff; lots of light easy food you can pick up on your way home from work and prepare without too much effort. I have a few pasta dishes in this section that use fresh pasta. Of course, you might not be making fresh pasta every time you have pasta for tea, but it's worth a try. It's easier than you think and the difference in the end dish between fresh and shop bought is incredible. I hope you will find this chapter helpful in making sure you avoid those nights in with convenience, processed foods.

3

21. Homemade pasta with meatballs
in a spicy tomato sauce

To make the pasta you have two options. One is with a food processor; the other is by hand. I prefer the food processor method as it's more consistent. This is a great supper to make the day before, as the flavours really intensify with time.

Pasta with a food processor

200 to 250g bread flour

2 eggs

1 tsp quality oil

1/2 tsp cold water

Pasta by hand

200g bread flour

2 eggs

1 tsp quality oil

1 tsp cold water

For the meatballs

1kg minced beef

4 shallots, finely diced

1 red chilli, finely diced

1 green chilli, finely diced

1 tbsp of dried mixed herbs

4 cloves of garlic, crushed

Salt and pepper

For the sauce

2 x 400g tins of chopped tomatoes

4 sticks celery, chopped small

1 red onion, diced

50g tomato purée

1 tsp chilli flakes

1 pinch dried mixed herbs

1 clove of garlic, crushed

1 tbsp sugar, to taste

1 lemon, juiced, to taste

Quality oil

Seasoning

Fresh pasta with a food processor

1. In a food processor place the eggs, oil and the cold water.
2. Start the machine and let it run for 2 minutes.
3. Gradually start adding the flour. It will start off being a very sticky dough. Keep adding the flour a little at a time until the dough breaks down and resembles uncooked couscous.
4. At this point turn off machine, take the mix out and begin to knead on your work surface, using as little flour as possible.
5. Once you have a smooth dough, wrap tightly in cling film and allow the pasta to rest.

Fresh pasta by hand

1. Sieve the flour into a bowl.
2. Beat the eggs with the oil.
3. Make a well in the centre of the flour and add the eggs and the oil.
4. Gradually incorporate the flour into the liquid.
5. Form into a dough, adding a little water if needed. And leave to rest.

Meatballs

1. Sweat all of the ingredients – except for the meat – in a pan with a touch of oil until softened but without colour.
2. Allow to cool, then add to the minced meat and season well.
3. Mould into small balls and allow to rest in the fridge for 30 minutes.

Sauce

1. Heat a heavy-bottomed pan and add a dash of oil. Add the chopped celery and diced red onion and sweat for 5 minutes without colouring.
2. Add the garlic and continue to cook for 1 minute before adding the tomatoes, the purée and the remaining ingredients.
3. Stir well and cook slowly for 30 minutes. Season to taste adding either the lemon juice or the sugar as required.
4. You can either leave the sauce coarse or blitz in a food processor for a smoother finish. Whichever you prefer! At this point you can add fresh herbs such as basil, marjoram or oregano if you like.
5. When you have made your sauce heat it in a pot. You can then pour it into a casserole dish and carefully add the meatballs, cover with a lid and bake in the oven for 2 hours at 130°C.
6. Serve with your pasta.

22. Pasta with hot smoked salmon,
fennel, broccoli, asparagus and chilli

400g pasta of your
  choice

200g hot smoked salmon

1 bulb of fennel

1 head of broccoli

2 red chillies

1/2 bunch of asparagus

1 bunch of baby spinach

1 lemon

75ml quality oil

Salt and cracked black
  pepper

This is such a nice simple dish, but the combination of salmon and asparagus feels like a truly luxurious one. I love how the hot smoked salmon is such a quick way of adding really bold, big flavours to your food.

1. Your first job is to get the pasta cooked. Fill a large pan with hot water and a good pinch of salt, then get it on the heat.

2. Once boiling, add a little oil and then your pasta. Set a timer using the instructions on the packet.

3. Once the pasta is cooked, drain through a colander, then pop the pasta back in the pot. Place the empty colander on top of the pot and put the whole lot under a running tap.

4. When completely cooled, drain back through the colander, allow to drip for a few minutes then pour some quality oil over the top.

5. Blanch and refresh your asparagus and broccoli and cut into manageable sizes.

6. Slice your fennel as thinly as you can. If you have a mandolin use that, a speed peeler also works.

7. Peel your lemon with a peeler. The aim is to remove as much of the white pith as you can, then cut the yellow rind as super finely as you can.

8. Finely slice your chillies.

9. Reheat your pasta by placing into a pan of boiling water for a couple of minutes.

10. In a wok or large pan add the broccoli, fennel, chilli, shredded lemon zest and asparagus with the oil.

11. Once it starts to heat up, add the spinach and the salmon.

12. Mix well, season with a squeeze of lemon juice and plenty of cracked black pepper. Serve immediately.

23. **Warm salmon** with pickled cucumber and mango salsa

4 x 125g salmon
  escalopes

30g fresh ginger, finely
  diced or grated

1 red chilli, finely diced

2 tbsp honey

2 tbsp soy sauce

1 tbsp toasted sesame oil

2 cloves of garlic, crushed

1 tsp sunflower oil

1 lime, juiced

For the salsa

1 mango, ripe

1 spring onion, sliced

1 lime, juiced

1/2 red chilli, finely
  chopped

1 bunch of basil leaves

Splash of sesame oil

For the cucumber

1/2 cucumber

1 lime, juiced

1 tsp honey

This is a very easy dish to make. You can replace the salmon with king prawns if you wish. It's a good idea to make the salsa while you're waiting for the salmon to marinate – then it'll be ready when the salmon is fresh from the pan.

1. Place the salmon into a bowl. Mix together all the other ingredients (except the oil) and pour over the salmon. Cover and marinate for 30 minutes.

2. It's important not to marinate any longer, as the salmon will start to cook.

3. Heat a non-stick frying pan with a teaspoon of sunflower oil.

4. Take the salmon out of the marinade and place into the hot pan.

5. The salmon will almost instantly start to caramelise and become black around the edges.

6. Cook for 1 to 2 minutes over a medium heat then turn and cook for a further 2 minutes.

Mango salsa

1. To start you will need to peel the mango. To do this, cut the top and bottom off the mango, place the mango on its end and peel a little at a time from top to bottom moving around until all the mango has been peeled.

2. The next thing I do is cut half-inch thick slices off the mango. You will need to cut until you reach the big flat stone in the middle. Do the same on the other side the same way and then you can get a couple of little slices from around the stone.

3. Cut the slices into ½ cm strips and then dice.

4. Mix the mango with all remaining ingredients.

5. Double check the seasoning.

Pickled cucumber

1. This is an instant pickle recipe, done at the last minute as the cucumber discolours and wilts very quickly once the lime juice is added.

2. The first job is to make the lime and honey pickle. It's just a case of mixing the two ingredients together until you create the right balance between sweet and sour.

3. Next take a peeler and cut ribbons from the cucumber, but only peeling until you reach the seeds.

4. Just before you are ready to serve, mix the sweet and sour honey and lime mixture with the cucumber ribbons and serve.

24. Wild mushroom and spinach frittata

4 to 6 eggs, beaten
75g wild mushrooms,
  roughly chopped
50g baby spinach
20g butter
20g Parmesan, grated
Seasoning

This is a fabulously quick recipe. The number of eggs you'll need is based on how big your frying pan is.

1. Heat your non-stick frying pan, then once it's warm add the butter and stir in the mushrooms.
2. Once the mushrooms are cooked add the spinach.
3. Allow the spinach to wilt down a little.
4. Add the beaten eggs and slowly mix the eggs, mushrooms and spinach together in the pan.
5. Top with the Parmesan and place into a hot oven at 180°C.
6. Cook for 5 to 6 minutes or until the eggs have set. Season to taste and serve.

25. Pan seared mackerel, purple sprouting broccoli, asparagus and cherry tomatoes

8 fillets of mackerel
1 pack of purple sprouting broccoli, or regular if purple sprouting is out of season
1 bunch of asparagus
250g cherry tomatoes
25ml quality oil
Salt and pepper

Mackerel! I love it: it's sustainable, healthy, very high in omega 3, easy to prepare, great value and jam-packed with flavour. I feel it's the most underrated fish out there and we should all be eating more of it.

1. To start, blanch and refresh the broccoli and the asparagus.
2. Cut the cherry tomatoes in half.
3. Cut the broccoli and the asparagus into smaller pieces.
4. Pop your grill on to a medium heat.
5. Place your fillets of mackerel onto a tray skin side up, brush with a little oil and place under the grill.
6. Place a frying pan onto the stove with a little oil and pop in the blanched broccoli, asparagus and the cherry tomatoes.
7. Season with a pinch of salt and a few turns of black pepper.
8. Once the fish is cooked and the vegetables are nice and hot, you are ready to serve.

26. Pesto chilli pasta

2 red chillies, finely chopped

2 shallots, finely chopped

70g basil, picked and washed

100g Parmesan

50g pine nuts

2 cloves of garlic

2 tbsp quality oil

Salt, to taste

For the pasta

1 batch of fresh pasta, see page 61, or

300g of dried pasta

This is one of the tastiest dishes in the book. It's very easy to make your own pesto and the difference from shop bought is night and day. The key ingredient is the basil – remember that you don't store basil in the fridge unlike most herbs. Make as much or as little as you need; pesto keeps very well in the fridge as long as it's in an airtight container topped with a little oil.

1. This is a really relaxed recipe! So, don't bother weighing out the basil. If you have two packets or a growing plant then get them used up. It's so relaxed in fact that you can happily change the cheese and the nuts to something different or to something you already have.

2. To get started, put your basil in a blender (or use a hand-held blender) with half the oil and a pinch of salt.

3. Add the pine nuts and then blend in the garlic.

4. Finally add 50g of the Parmesan or cheese of your choice and blend with the rest of the oil. Your pesto is now made.

5. The next job is to cook the pasta. If you are cooking dried follow the packet instructions, which will normally advise 10 to 12 minutes. The only exception I have to this is spaghetti. I feel it eats and holds the sauce much better when it's overcooked. Try it yourself next time – you might get a pleasant surprise.

6. Next put the shallots and the chopped chilli into your pan and slowly soften down on a medium heat with a little oil.

7. Strain your pasta and put directly into the pan with the shallots and chilli.

8. Next add the pesto – be generous – and top with Parmesan shavings.

27. **Crab pasta** with chilli, spinach, asparagus and red onion

For the pasta

1 batch of fresh pasta, see page 61, *or*

300g of dried pasta

For the crab, to finish

150g crab meat

1 bunch of asparagus, blanched, refreshed

1 red chilli, finely chopped

1 red onion, thinly sliced

70g baby spinach, picked, washed and shredded

2 cloves of garlic, crushed

2 tbsp quality oil

1 lemon, juiced

This is a fantastic, tasty dish. Crab is an ingredient that many home cooks won't have used before. It is relatively easy to get a hold of – a good fishmonger should stock it, or your local Asian supermarket if you are lucky enough to have one nearby. Crab provides big flavour without any real effort. One thing to remember is that the crab meat when you buy it is normally cooked; so be careful when making this dish not to overheat it and ruin the texture.

1. The first job is to prepare the asparagus, garlic, chilli and red onion.
2. Blanch and refresh your asparagus and cut into slices.
3. Next put the red onion and the chopped chilli into your pan and slowly soften down on a medium heat with a little oil.
4. The next job is to cook the pasta. If you are cooking dried pasta then follow the instructions on the pack.
5. Strain your pasta and put directly into the pan with the onion and chilli.
6. Next add the shredded spinach and the asparagus.
7. The last thing you need to add is the crab meat. Mix it through and ensure the whole dish is piping hot.
8. Double check the seasoning and finish with a little squeeze of lemon juice.

28. Pesto pasta with mushrooms and Mediterranean vegetables

400g pasta, of your choice

1 red onion, sliced

1 courgette, diced

1 pack of chestnut mushrooms

1 red pepper, sliced

1 aubergine, cut into chunks

25g tomato purée

1 tin of chopped tomatoes

1 tsp dried oregano

2 cloves of garlic, chopped

50g Parmesan

50ml quality oil

Salt and sugar, to taste

For the pesto
See recipe on page 138

This as a super simple supper, a cook on the night straight from work kind of dish. The vegetables are up to you; just use whatever you have. If you have a batch of pesto premade all the better. Remember, you can even precook the pasta.

1. First job is to get the pasta cooked. So, fill a large pan with water, a good pinch of salt and get it on the heat.

2. Once boiling, add a little oil and then your pasta. Set a timer using the instructions on the packet. When using spaghetti, I actually overcook it as I find the sauce sticks better and it eats much better; give it a go – see what you think.

3. Once the pasta is cooked, drain through a colander, pop the pasta back in the pot, place the empty colander on top of the pot and place the whole lot under a running tap.

4. When completely cooled, drain back through the colander, allow to drip for a few minutes then pour quality oil over the top. Pasta can be precooked and stored in the fridge for a day.

5. Now start preparing your vegetables, keeping your garlic separate.

6. The secret to real flavour in this simple dish is to cook the vegetables first in a hot pan. I would probably cook them one at a time, giving them plenty of colour. When you cook like this you are removing lots of the water from the vegetables and thus enhancing their flavour.

7. Once all your vegetables have been coloured, get them all back into the same pan, add the oregano, chopped garlic and cook for a few seconds.

8. Add the tin of tomatoes and the tomato purée, and combine. Add salt and sugar to taste.

9. Reheat your pasta by placing it into a pan of boiling water for a couple of minutes.

10. Add the hot pasta to the vegetables, with a tablespoon of pesto and mix.

11. Serve topped with shavings of Parmesan or other hard cheese, plus a few more spoonfuls of fresh pesto to taste.

29. Lemon sole tempura with pickled vegetables

4 fillets of lemon sole, cut into strips

100g plain flour, plus a little extra to coat the fish before it goes in to the batter

150ml ice water

20ml rice wine vinegar

75g cornflour

1 egg yolk

Baking powder

Sesame oil, for frying

Pinch of salt

Pinch of sugar

For the pickled vegetables

2 baby carrots

2 asparagus spears

1 red chilli

1 golden beetroot

1/4 cucumber

150ml rice wine vinegar

150g sugar

2 sprigs of thyme

The combination of crispy fried fish and pickle is a British classic; this is a little twist on that. Any non-oily fish will fry well in batter. Tempura batter is super crispy and light and is very simple to make and get right. Prepare the vegetables first so they have time to pickle nicely while you cook the fish.

Lemon sole tempura

1. Put the vinegar, egg yolk, sugar and water into a bowl.
2. Sieve the flour, cornflour, baking powder and salt into the water and the vinegar, then with a whisk gradually incorporate until you have a smooth batter. You might have to thin down with a little water to achieve a coating consistency.
3. When you are ready to fry the fish heat your oil up to about 180°C in a wok. You'll find that doing this in a wok is much safer than a pot as it has a very wide rim that is unlikely to spill over.
4. Take your strips of fish and dip in a little flour before coating them in batter. The reason for this is that the flour will stick to the fish and the batter will stick to the flour giving you a nice even coating.
5. Carefully – and one strip at a time – deep fry the fish until golden brown.

Pickled vegetables

1. Using a mandolin or a speed peeler cut your vegetables into thin strips.
2. In a pot boil your vinegar, sugar and thyme.
3. Once it has boiled remove from the heat and add your raw sliced vegetables.
4. The longer you leave them in this vinegar liquid the more pickled they will become.

30. Seared squid with salsa verde and spicy wedges

800g fresh squid,
  small to medium

1 red chilli

1 green chilli

50ml quality oil

Cajun spice

1/2 tsp paprika

1/2 bunch of flat parsley

4 medium Maris Piper
  potatoes

2 tsp semolina, optional

1 lemon

Salt and fresh cracked
  black pepper

For the salsa verde
See recipe on page 140

I absolutely love squid. It's quick, easy, good value and when it's done right is tender and tasty. This dish is lovely and simple, just as it should be. I like to get the cleaner jobs out the way before starting on the messy ones.

1. The first job is to get your spicy wedges started. Pop your potatoes into a preheated oven at 180°C for about 40 minutes to an hour, just until the potatoes have cooked. This can be done in advance or, if you are in a real hurry, in the microwave.

2. The next job is to prepare the chillies. Top and tail each chilli, split in half, remove the seeds and the pith. Cut each half into very thin strips and then dice each strip finely.

3. With the parsley give it a wash then pick the leaves off the stalks, and in small bunches roll up the leaves and shred finely. Flat parsley is much better if it has just been shredded and not chopped.

4. Zest and halve the lemon.

5. If your potatoes are cooked and cooled a little, cut them in half then cut each half into wedges. Next place onto a tray, coat in oil and dust with Cajun spice and semolina. The semolina is great for giving the wedges a little bit more of a crunch.

6. You can shallow fry or bake the wedges in a hot oven at around 210°C.

7. Now onto the squid. Don't be put off working with squid – it's very easy. One thing you need to be sure of is that it's the freshest squid possible. It should be relatively clean and have a pleasant smell.

8. The first job with the squid is to remove the tentacles. To do this hold the squid tube in your left hand and with your right hand grip it right at the point it meets the tube, and pull. This will also remove most of the innards.

9. Cut the tentacles away from the eye and the innards by cutting right at the point the eye meets the tentacles.

10. You should now have the tentacles separated. There's just one more job with the tentacles, which is to remove the beak from the centre of the tentacles.

11. Now onto the squid tube itself. First, remove the outer skin if it has any and the two wings.

12. Next turn the squid inside out and give it a clean. Make sure you remove the transparent spine and give it all a good clean.

continues on the next page

30. Seared squid with salsa verde and spicy wedges

13. You will now notice that the squid tube has a seam running from top to bottom. Using your knife or a pair of scissors cut along this line. This will open up the squid. Next you need to establish which is the soft side, once you have done this, then score the squid making sure you don't cut all the way through.

14. Place the cut squid and the tentacles into a bowl with some oil, about a tablespoon of Cajun spice, the paprika, diced chillies, lemon zest and some seasoning.

15. Place your pan or skillet onto the heat, get it as hot as you dare, pour a little oil into the pan then, cut side down first, place in the squid tubes flat as you can. Once all the tubes are in add the tentacles. Don't shake or shoogle the pan until the squid is almost cooked and then with a pair of tongs peel the squid from the bottom of the pan.

16. The squid should spring inside out to reveal the cut edge.

17. Finish by adding the parsley and lemon juice.

18. Serve with your spiced wedges and your salsa verde.

Pan seared salmon with salad and sweet potato fries

31. Pan seared salmon with a chickpea, green chilli salad and sweet potato fries

4 x 150g salmon fillets
1 tin of chickpeas, drained
1 green chilli
1 bunch of coriander
150ml Greek yogurt
1/2 tsp coriander seeds
25g butter
1 lemon, zested and juiced
Cooking oil
Smoked paprika, for dusting

For the sweet potato fries
See recipe on page 150

This is a very light, easy dish to prepare. The toasted coriander seeds give the chickpea salad a real lift and this salad combination works with almost anything.

1. The first task is to get the sweet potato fries sorted. See page 150.
2. The next job is to make the chickpea chilli salad. Finely dice the green chilli, shred the coriander and put in a bowl with the yogurt and chickpeas.
3. Toast the coriander seeds in a dry frying pan: heat until the seeds start to colour and crackle, remove from the pan to cool then pop into a sandwich bag and crush slightly with a rolling pin. Finally, add to the yogurt mixture.
4. Grate some lemon zest into the mix and then the juice of half a lemon, next dust in some smoked paprika.
5. Taste for seasoning and then put to one side.
6. The next task is to cook the salmon. Preheat your oven to 200°C.
7. Pop a frying pan onto the heat, add a little oil to the pan and heat up.
8. Once hot place your salmon fillets skin-side down into the hot pan.
9. The important thing to do next is not to touch, poke or prod the fish. Yes, your fish is stuck to the pan – it's meant to be. Leave it alone; it will unstick itself as the skin becomes crisper.
10. After a few minutes carefully try to lift the fish. Use a dessert spoon at the edge of the skin and see if it can be removed from the bottom of the pan easily.
11. Controlling the temperature at this stage is critical. Listen to the noise of the fish cooking as it tells you what is going on in the pan. It should be making a happy sizzling sound. If the pan is making loads of noise and spitting fat everywhere it's too hot – turn it down.
12. Flip the salmon over onto each side and the bottom to create a little colour.
13. Once the fish has been sealed on all sides remove from the pan and pop onto a tray and dust with paprika and a little bit of butter on top of each fillet.
14. Place into your preheated oven and cook for 4 minutes.
15. Remove from the oven and rest for about 4 minutes.
16. You are now ready to serve.

32. Citrus garlic prawns with giant couscous pomegranate salad

For the prawns

12 large raw prawns, shells off

2 cloves of garlic, crushed

1 lime, juiced

1/2 lemon, juiced

2 red chillies, deseeded and finely chopped

1 tbsp quality oil

1 tbsp honey

For the salad

1 pomegranate, large

200g giant couscous, sometimes known as Israeli or pearl couscous

250ml chicken stock, boiling

2 limes, juice and zest from one

6 tbsp of quality oil

Fresh coriander and mint, to garnish

Salt and freshly ground black pepper, to season

With this recipe you need to marinate the prawns. Always be careful not to marinate fish and shellfish too long as it can start to cook, which isn't what you want. You can make the couscous salad while the prawns marinate.

Citrus garlic prawns

1. In a shallow dish mix together the garlic, lime and lemon juices, chillies, oil and honey.
2. Add the prawns, season with black pepper and marinate in the fridge for 30 minutes.
3. Place the prawns onto a hot griddle pan until pink and cooked, basting them with any leftover marinade.
4. Serve with the couscous salad.

Giant couscous salad

1. Cut the pomegranate in half and knock out the seeds using a wooden spoon by placing the cut side of the fruit down and hitting the skin hard with the spoon. This will remove the seeds, leaving the white membrane in the skin.
2. Place the couscous in a pan. Pour on the boiling stock (or water) and mix in the oil and lime juice. Cook out slowly until the couscous is soft and has taken on all the stock.
3. Season with salt and freshly ground black pepper.
4. Once the couscous is cooled add the mint, lime zest, coriander and pomegranate seeds.

33. Lamb tagine with almonds and bell peppers

400g lamb shoulder, evenly diced

1 tin of chickpeas, drained and rinsed

1 red onion, sliced

400g tin of chopped tomatoes

8 cherry tomatoes, cut into halves

1 red pepper, cut into large dice

1/2 tsp garlic, chopped

2 tsp curry powder

1/2 tsp ground coriander

1/2 tsp ground cumin

1 bay leaf

50g flaked almonds

Small dried chilli flakes, optional

Sprinkle of plain white flour

It's lovely to use a traditional Moroccan tagine for this recipe – they have a great earthenware texture and look good on the table – but any large dish with a snug lid will do. This also works as a veggie dish. You can substitute the lamb with butternut squash, courgette or aubergine.

1. Preheat the oven to 160°C.
2. As you'll see, this is probably one of the easiest dishes in the book! Once you have chopped all the vegetables pop them into a large bowl.
3. Then add the diced lamb and the spices, including chilli flakes if you like.
4. Next add the tin of tomatoes, rinse out the tomato tin with 100ml of water and add to the base mix.
5. Drain and rinse the chickpeas and add them to the mix.
6. Dust with a teaspoon of flour and then give the whole lot a really good mix.
7. Place the ingredients in the middle of the tagine or your pot with a tight-fitting lid. Put the lid on and cook in the oven for about 2 hours or until the lamb is tender.
8. Remove carefully from the oven and let it stand for about 15 minutes.
9. Top with the sliced almonds and serve.

34. Roast fillet of cod with a curried mussel and vegetable stew

4 x 160g cod fillets

1kg fresh mussels in shell

3 banana shallots, finely diced

1 courgette, diced into 1 cm pieces

1/2 leek, diced

1 bulb fennel, diced

1/2 tsp cayenne pepper

2 tsp curry powder

1 tsp turmeric

1 tsp ground coriander

1 tsp ground cumin

3 cloves of garlic, chopped

Piece of ginger, finely chopped or grated

1 tin of coconut milk

100ml double cream

1 tsp tamarind paste

200ml chicken stock, a quality cube will work

Cooking oil

A knob of butter

Salt and pepper, to taste

This is a beautiful dish with the delicate fish and mussels complemented by the rich fragrant flavours of the curry. You will need to prepare the mussels first. See recipe 8 on page 37 for the best way to do this.

1. To start take a large pot and add a little oil, then add the shallots. Cook them without colouring and next add the prepared mussels and cook with a little chicken stock. The mussels should only take a few minutes until they have opened.

2. Pass the mussels through a colander into a bowl; reserve the cooking liquor as this will form the base of the sauce.

3. Once cool enough to handle pick the mussels from the shells; if any mussels haven't opened discard them. Reserve a few mussels in the shell for a garnish at the end.

4. In a large pan, add the garlic and ginger and sweat in a little oil for a few minutes, then add all the spices.

5. The next thing into the pot is the diced vegetables. Now cook until the vegetables are softened.

6. Add the mussel stock and reduce, this will help cook out the spices.

7. Next add the coconut milk, cream and tamarind paste and reduce until thickened. The sauce should now start to taste good.

8. You can now look at cooking the cod. Preheat your oven to 180°C. Pop a frying pan onto the heat, add a little oil to the pan and heat up.

9. Once hot place your cod fillets skin-side down into the hot pan.

10. The important thing to do next is not to touch, poke or prod the fish. Leave it alone and it will unstick itself as the skin becomes crisper.

11. After a few minutes carefully try and lift the fish. Use a dessert spoon at the edge of the skin and see if it can be removed from the bottom of the pan easily.

12. Controlling the temperature at this stage is critical: listen to the noise of the fish cooking. It tells you loads about what is going on in the pan; it should be making a happy sizzling sound. If the pan is making loads of noise and spitting fat everywhere then it's too hot and you need to turn it down.

13. Flip the cod over onto each side and the bottom to create a little colour all round the fish.

14. Once the fish has been sealed on all sides remove from the pan and pop onto a tray. Add a bit of butter on top of each fillet.

15. Cook the cod for about 6 minutes in the oven. Then allow the fish to rest for about 6 minutes once it comes out the oven.

16. Add the picked mussels into the curried vegetable stew and enjoy.

ALL THINGS SPICE

What is it about spicy food that we love so much? In the UK curry is almost the national dish, and I love the big flavours of spice; they can turn the most ordinary ingredient into something truly special. In this chapter there is a wide range of food from different cultures and methods. Please use the ingredient amounts stated here as a guide as everyone tastes spice differently. You could always ask – what is a half a teaspoon anyway? I believe the best way to learn how to cook with spice is to cook with spice. I know that doesn't sound desperately helpful, but the more you work with spices the better you understand how much is needed to make a positive difference to the dish. Think about each spice differently as they all do a unique job, and remember that most spices have no heat in them at all. I would also advise you to use whole spices – the best way is to toast and grind them as you need them as the smell and flavour you create by doing this is incredible. Using a pestle and mortar for grinding spices is very satisfying and if you're lucky it'll make you look windswept and interesting to your neighbours.

I have recently visited Asia – Malaysia, Singapore, India and most recently Indonesia – and the food culture there is incredible; life truly revolves around food. When I encounter amazing tastes I just want to get home and re-create them. If you cook a lot of Asian-themed food then of course it makes sense to seek out your nearest Asian shop as the range is often incredible, and it is always cheaper and more enjoyable than buying branded names in the supermarkets. I often go in to find stuff I have never seen before just so I can try it out – and if I can't read the label, even better. I have made some fabulous discoveries along the way. Where I live I am lucky to have a huge Asian supermarket full of amazing, authentic ingredients, which means that as soon as I get back from a trip to Asia it's always my first stop.

My top tips are to be bold with spice, learn what effect each spice has on food, and remember that the more you cook with spice the better you will become at understanding each one.

35. Chicken paella with king prawns and mussels

6 chicken thighs

16 king prawns

1kg mussels, washed and de-bearded

250g cherry tomatoes, halved

4 plum tomatoes, quartered and chopped

250g paella rice

Pinch of saffron

1 bunch of flat parsley, shredded

1 litre of chicken stock, quality stock cubes are ideal

2 cloves of garlic, finely sliced

20ml quality oil

1 tsp smoked paprika

Salt and pepper

There are so many variations on paella, with some arguing that meat and fish shouldn't be mixed; others will use chorizo rather than chicken. The saffron adds a gorgeous reddish hue to this take on the one-pot classic.

1. Heat a non-stick frying pan, add a tablespoon of oil then add the chicken and colour lightly over a medium heat for about 6 to 8 minutes.

2. Now add the prawns and mussels. See recipe 8 on page 37 for how to prepare mussels.

3. Next add the garlic and cook for 1 minute.

4. Sprinkle over the chopped tomatoes and allow to soften, shaking the pan several times.

5. Now add the rice and saffron.

6. Pour over the stock, shake the pan and then add the paprika. Simmer for 15 to 20 minutes, shaking the pan every so often.

7. Five minutes before the end of the cooking time add the shredded parsley and cherry tomatoes, checking that the chicken is cooked through.

8. Double check the seasoning and serve.

36. Hot smoked salmon kedgeree
with quail eggs and mussels

200g hot smoked salmon

300g mussels, fresh

200ml white wine

12 quail eggs

Small bunch of flat parsley, shredded

Small bunch of coriander, shredded

A few sprigs of dill

25ml vegetable oil

2 banana shallots, chopped

1 onion, sliced

50g butter

1 tsp ground coriander

1 tsp ground turmeric

2 tsp curry powder

1 bay leaf

250g long grain rice

Salt and pepper, to taste

Spicy, warming and fabulous, kedgeree is always a winner. This recipe is a variant on the usual haddock, using salmon and mussels. You will need to clean and prepare the mussels before starting, but once you have mastered this skill you might be tempted to cook mussels at home quite often. You'll need a large pan with a tight-fitting lid to cook the mussels.

1. Your first job is to clean the mussels. Wash them under cold running water, then – using a table knife – scrape away any barnacles. You also have to remove the beard: pull out any beards that protrude from between the closed shells.

2. If you find any mussels are open, give them a short little tap on the side of the sink; this should encourage them to close. If they don't close they should be thrown away as they are most likely dead.

3. Now place the cleaned mussels into a bowl and add the chopped shallots, butter, salt, pepper and wine.

4. My method for cooking mussels is to cook them very, very quickly. See recipe 8 on page 37 for how to do this.

5. Once the mussels are cooked, strain the cooking liquors and set to one side, then pick the meat from the shells.

6. To cook the rice, first heat the oil in a large, lidded pan, add the onion, then gently fry for 5 minutes until softened but not coloured.

7. Add the bay leaf and spices, season with salt, then fry until the mix starts to go brown and fragrant; this will take about 3 minutes.

8. Add the rice and stir in well.

9. Add 200ml of water and the mussel cooking liquor, stir and bring to the boil.

10. Reduce to a simmer and cover for 10 minutes.

11. Meanwhile, place the quail eggs in a pan of boiling water and cook for 2.5 minutes. This will give you a runny egg yolk; if you'd prefer not-so-runny then simply cook for a little longer.

12. Take off the heat and leave to stand, covered, for another 10 to 15 minutes.

13. The rice will be cooked to perfection – as long as you don't lift the lid off the pan before the end of the cooking.

14. Fold through the salmon, mussels and fresh herbs.

15. Finish with the quail eggs cut into neat quarters and a few sprigs of dill.

37. Italian sausage risotto
with pea and parsley

4 Italian sausages

240g Arborio rice

2 shallots, finely diced

4 cloves of garlic, finely minced

1/4 bunch of flat parsley

50g butter

650ml chicken stock, a stock cube is good

25g Parmesan, in a block

150ml white wine

150g peas

Salt

I think the home cook can make a better risotto than most restaurants. This bold statement is based on the fact that a risotto is always best when cooked and eaten straight away. Some restaurants half cook the rice so it's quicker to serve when an order comes in. Restaurants also struggle with the 20 minutes of labour needed to stir a risotto. The more stirring the better. It's the starch in the rice that makes a risotto creamy – not cream! Use the best quality sausage you can: it will be full of flavour and do loads of the work in terms of seasoning and enjoyment of the dish.

1. Heat a sauté pan or pot and add half of the butter, then add the shallots and garlic and sweat for 3 to 4 minutes without it colouring.

2. Remove the sausage from its skin, break it up and brown in the pan. Cook for 2 minutes.

3. Now add the rice; when you add the rice it's vital that you 'toast it'. This is done by cooking it out in the pan with the sausage and shallots and making sure that every grain of rice gets coated in the other ingredients. When you start to hear the rice crackle this is an indication that you have toasted the rice properly.

4. You are now ready to pour in the wine, and reduce until the wine has totally evaporated.

5. Start to add the stock a ladle at a time, making sure the previous stock has been fully absorbed. The real secret of making the best risotto is to continually stir with a non-metallic spoon while adding the stock. This elbow grease will make the risotto very light and creamy.

6. Continue this method until the rice is cooked; keep tasting and checking for how it's cooked and how it's seasoned until it's how you like it.

7. Double check seasoning, add peas and parsley. Finish with Parmesan and butter.

8. The consistency of the risotto should be like lava from a volcano; if you were to serve it on a plate it should run to the edges. If it's too thick it will be very heavy to eat.

38. Chicken katsu curry

For the sauce

1 onion, chopped

2 cloves of garlic, peeled

2 carrots, peeled and chopped

2 tbsp plain flour

1 tsp Madras curry powder

600ml chicken stock, use 2 stock cubes

2 tsp honey

1 tbsp soy sauce

1 bay leaf

1/2 tsp garam masala

Cooking oil

For the chicken

2 chicken breasts

2 slices of bread, crumbed

2 eggs

20ml milk

100g plain flour, seasoned

This Japanese classic with its knockout combination of crispy chicken and a rich sauce is a true restaurant favourite that you can make to order at home. The chicken is made using a pané system: a simple series of plates that enables you to add breadcrumbs to a piece of meat. Once you've mastered the logistics of this, you can use it to make pork escalopes, experiment with fish or even pieces of quorn. Try adding different seasonings to the flour too.

Sauce

1. To make the sauce, heat the oil in a small pan.
2. Add the chopped onion and garlic and sauté for 2 minutes, then add in the carrots and sweat slowly for 10 minutes with the lid on. Stir until the vegetables have softened and started to caramelise.
3. Stir in the flour and curry powder and cook for 1 minute.
4. Slowly pour in the stock until combined.
5. Add the honey, soy sauce and bay leaf and bring to the boil.
6. Reduce the heat and simmer for 20 minutes, so the sauce thickens but is still of pouring consistency.
7. Add the garam masala, then pass the sauce through a sieve.
8. Serve with your crispy chicken and sticky rice. See recipe on page 151.

Crispy chicken

1. Lay the chicken breasts flat on the chopping board. Place your hand on top of the chicken and carefully slice through to create two pieces of chicken.
2. The next thing to do is breadcrumb the chicken. To do this you will need what's called a pané system. This consists of a tray with seasoned flour, one with an egg and a little milk beaten together and a third tray with breadcrumbs.
3. Pass the chicken through the flour first, then the egg wash and lastly the breadcrumbs. The idea is that the flour will stick to the chicken, then the egg sticks to the flour and the crumbs stick to the egg wash.
4. To cook, shallow fry until golden and cooked through. Depending on how thick the chicken is it might need some time in the oven to cook through.

39. Beef rendang curry

600g blade or chuck
steak, cut into 2.5 to
4 cm pieces

400ml coconut milk

1/2 tsp soft brown sugar

Salt

Tamarind paste

For the dried spices

3 tbsp coriander seeds

2 tsp cumin seeds

1 cinnamon stick

1 clove

For the paste

4 red chillies

5 cm fresh ginger, peeled

4 cloves of garlic, finely
chopped

1 onion, roughly chopped

1 tsp turmeric

Rendang is a meltingly tender spicy beef dish, which originates from Indonesia. With its deep flavours and layers of spices, it more than earns its title as the king of curries. Like so many slow-cooked foods it gets better with time and the complexity really shines through if you eat it the day after you make it.

1. For the dried spices toast the seeds in a dry frying pan and then grind all the spices to a fine powder. A pestle and mortar is ideal for this.

2. Put the ginger, garlic, onion, chilli and turmeric in a food processor and blend to a smooth paste.

3. Sear the meat in a heavy-bottomed pan then tip the paste in and cook out for 2 to 3 minutes.

4. Now add the ground spices and cook for 30 seconds.

5. Add the tamarind paste, coconut milk, sugar and a pinch of salt.

6. Bring to a simmer, place the lid on the pan and cook for about 1 to 1½ hours in an oven set at 140°C. Give it a stir now and then.

7. Stir more frequently towards the end of cooking as the sauce becomes concentrated to stop it sticking.

8. Serve with coconut rice. See recipe on page 151.

40. Peshawari chicken curry

4 tbsp quality oil

1 cinnamon stick

4 green cardamom pods

4 cloves

1 bay leaf

1kg chicken thighs

1 large onion

50g ginger, puréed,
  with a Microplane grater

4 cloves of garlic, puréed

50g tomato purée

1 tsp ground turmeric

1 tsp ground coriander

1 tsp ground cumin

170g Greek yogurt

4 tsp gram flour

1 tsp chilli powder

175ml chicken stock, a
  stock cube is fine

Mint and coriander leaves,
  shredded

This fantastic recipe is so easy to do at home. I find chicken thighs give the dish a much better flavour, and they have the added bonus of not drying out when cooked long and slow. If you have a pressure cooker this dish only takes 20 minutes cooking time on the stove top.

1. In a medium pan, preferably with an ovenproof handle, heat the oil over a low heat. Add the cinnamon, cardamom, cloves and bay leaf.

2. Let them sizzle for 30 seconds, then add the chicken thighs, skin on or off, bone in or out, depending what you like. Increase the heat to medium-high and cook until the meat begins to brown and all the natural juices have evaporated.

3. Add the onion (sliced, not into rainbows, but the other way) and cook to a light golden colour for 4 to 5 minutes, then add the ginger and garlic purées for 30 seconds.

4. Add the tomato purée, turmeric, ground coriander and cumin. Continue to cook the spices for 3 to 4 minutes.

5. Whisk together the yogurt, gram flour and the chilli powder and add to the meat.

6. Now reduce the heat to low, add the stock, check for seasoning, cover and cook in the oven at 130°C until the meat is tender. This will take about 1½ to 2 hours.

7. Once tender stir in the fresh mint and the coriander. Serve – it's fabulous with the rice of your choice or naan bread.

41. King prawn and monkfish curry
with pilaf rice and pomegranate raita

For the curry

250g monkfish

500g king prawns

3 banana shallots, finely diced

1/2 tsp cayenne pepper

1 tsp paprika

1 tsp turmeric

1 tsp ground coriander

1 tsp ground cumin

3 cloves of garlic, chopped

Piece of ginger, finely chopped or grated

1 tin coconut milk

100ml double cream

1 tsp tamarind paste

200ml chicken stock, a quality cube works well

Salt and pepper

Cooking oil

For the pomegranate raita

250ml natural yogurt

1 pomegranate

1/2 bunch of coriander, shredded

1 red chilli

1/2 tsp garam masala

Subtle and creamy, this fish-based curry is a special, delicious thing. Like most curries, it feels incomplete without yogurt to cool the palate. Here is an extravagant kind of raita – the pomegranate seeds add a lovely sweet flavour.

Curry

1. To start, take a large pot and add a little oil. Now add the chopped shallots and cook without colouring.

2. Next add garlic and ginger and sweat for a further few minutes. Then add all the spices. You'll notice that the kitchen will start to fill with the most wonderful smells.

3. Add the chicken stock and reduce; this helps cook out the spices.

4. Next add the coconut milk, cream and tamarind paste and reduce until thickened. The sauce should now start to taste really good.

5. Add the monkfish and cook for a few minutes. Then add the king prawns.

6. Poach in the sauce until the fish is perfectly cooked.

7. Serve with raita and a portion of delicate pilaf rice – see recipe on page 152.

Pomegranate raita

1. Cut the pomegranate in half and knock out the seeds using a wooden spoon. You do this by placing the cut side of the fruit down and hitting the skin hard with the spoon. This will remove the seeds to leave the white membrane in the skin.

2. Mix the pomegranate seeds with the shredded coriander, diced chilli, garam masala and yogurt.

42. Ramen with noodles, pork belly, chestnut mushrooms, seaweed, spring onions, bean sprouts and a boiled egg

300g ramen noodles

250g pork belly, sliced 2 cm thick

50g ginger, finely diced or grated

2 cloves of garlic, finely chopped

2 chestnut mushrooms, sliced

1 tbsp toasted sesame oil

1 tbsp chilli bean paste, Doubanjiang is best

1/2 tsp dried bonito flakes

For the broth

300ml brown chicken stock

1 tsp Japanese miso paste

1 tsp soy sauce

1.5 tbsp rice vinegar

2 spring onions, sliced

For the toppings

2 eggs, hard boiled

1 sheet nori seaweed, pre-packed

50g bean sprouts

1 bunch of fresh coriander

1 red chilli, sliced

There are many variations on the classic ramen dish – noodles, a dark broth and a selection of toppings. There's no need for the takeaway menu when you can create your own. Experiment as the mood takes you.

1. In a medium saucepan, heat the sesame oil over a medium-high heat and add the ginger and garlic when the oil is hot.

2. When fragrant, add the chilli bean paste and stir.

3. Now add the pork and cook until it takes on some colour.

4. Add the chestnut mushrooms and cook until wilted.

5. Next add water or stock and bring to a boil.

6. Lower the heat to medium-low and add miso and soy sauce to the broth and simmer for 5 minutes.

7. Add the chopped spring onions and rice vinegar. Turn off the heat and set aside.

8. Cook the noodles in boiling salted water. When done, drain completely and place in ice-cold water.

9. Divide the noodles between your plates or bowls. Serve all the toppings on the noodles or onto a separate plate.

10. Pour the hot soup in a bowl. Serve the cold noodles, toppings, and soup and sprinkle bonito flakes in the soup right before enjoying.

HEART WARMERS

We all love home-cooked food – and in this chapter are some of my family favourites. Loads of these recipes are British classics: nothing complicated, dishes my gran would have cooked, the sort of food that encourages people to get around the table. I would serve most of these dishes buffet style and let people help themselves – there's nothing better than being the first person to crack open a fish pie or a baked mac 'n' cheese. Some of the best plates of food you will ever eat are the simplest and, for me, one of the best recipes is a simple roast chicken: done properly it's an incredible dish. This is the sort of family food that makes people smile, recognisable simple creations. It's the type of food my kids will ask for, and so I often cook these dishes at home. Some will take a little planning and almost all of them can be pre-done if you are organised enough to do some batch cooking.

5

43. Mac 'n' cheese
with smoked bacon and leek

For the white sauce
50g butter
50g plain flour, sifted
500ml milk
1 bay leaf
2 cloves
1 small onion
50g Cheddar, grated
50g Parmesan, grated

For the macaroni
250g macaroni
2 leeks, finely sliced
150g smoked bacon or
  pancetta, diced
30g Cheddar, grated
30g Parmesan, grated
4 tbsp white breadcrumbs
1 tsp cooking oil
Salt and pepper, to taste

Mac 'n' cheese is perhaps the ultimate comfort food – rich, creamy, heartening and irresistible. There are many ways to make it – some people swear by the addition of mustard – but I love the sweet flavour of the leeks in this one. You can always leave out the bacon to create a veggie version. Either way, it's a great standalone.

White sauce

1. The first job is to peel your onion. Then, using the cloves, pierce the bay leaf onto the onion. Place the studded onion into a small pot and cover with the milk.
2. Slowly bring the milk up to a simmer. As soon as the milk is simmering turn off the heat and allow the studded onion to flavour the milk.
3. Melt the butter in another small pan, then add flour and mix to form a thick paste called a roux.
4. Cook for 3 to 4 minutes, then slowly start to add the warm, flavoured milk. Stir continuously while milk is added until you achieve a smooth sauce with the consistency of thick double cream. If you add the milk a little at a time you will avoid your sauce turning lumpy.
5. Cook for 10 minutes over a very low heat to avoid burning the sauce, stirring every minute or so. Gradually add the cheese as you go.
6. Once cooked cover with cling film or parchment paper to avoid it forming a skin.

Macaroni

1. Heat the oil in a large, lidded pan over a low heat. Add the leeks and diced bacon, cover and cook for 10 minutes until tender.
2. Meanwhile, cook the macaroni in a large pan of boiling salted water for 10 minutes – as per the pack instructions – until just cooked. It shouldn't be completely cooked as it will continue to cook when baked.
3. Drain and set aside. Preheat the oven to 190°C.
4. Add your sauce to your cooked leeks and bacon, add the cooked pasta to the sauce then place into an ovenproof baking dish.
5. Top with cheese and scatter the breadcrumbs over the top.
6. Bake in the oven for 20 to 25 minutes until golden and bubbling around the edges. Serve immediately – with a little green salad if you fancy it.

44. Steak pie

900g stewing steak,
  cut into cubes

20g seasoned flour

1 tbsp olive oil

2 onions, sliced

1 tbsp parsley, chopped

1 tbsp thyme, chopped

Salt and freshly ground
  black pepper

500ml hot beef stock

225g/8oz puff pastry,
  ready-made

1 egg, beaten

There's not many things better than a classic homemade steak pie. This one uses shop-bought puff pastry – there's rarely any reason to make this yourself. Ready-made pastry can be kept in the freezer, which is super handy.

1. Dust the cubed steak with the seasoned flour. You can do this in a zip-lock bag or simply turn it over in a big bowl.

2. Heat the oil in a large heavy-bottomed pan and fry the meat, remembering not to shake the pan or to stir the meat until it has browned on that side.

3. Once the meat has browned on all sides, add the sliced onions, herbs, salt, freshly ground black pepper and the stock and bring to the boil.

4. Reduce the heat and simmer gently for an hour and a half until the meat is tender.

5. Preheat the oven to 190°C.

6. Transfer the filling mixture to an ovenproof dish.

7. Cut a piece of pastry and roll it out to fit across the top of the dish pressing the edges together to seal.

8. Make a steam hole in the centre of the pie by slashing with a sharp knife, then brush with beaten egg.

9. Transfer to the oven and cook until the pastry is golden and crisp – which should take about 40 minutes.

45. Fish pie

1 pack of fish pie mix, between 320g to 400g

50g butter

50g plain flour

500ml milk

1 bay leaf

2 cloves

1 small onion

150g Cheddar, grated

50g Parmesan, grated

4 spring onions, finely sliced

1 tsp Dijon or English mustard

25g chives, finely snipped

100g frozen sweetcorn

100g frozen peas

Salt and pepper, to taste

For the mashed potato
See recipe on page 147

A classic fish pie is filling and full of flavour. The fish mix you use can include cod, salmon, smoked haddock and so on – it's up to you.

1. The first job is to peel your onion, then, using the cloves, pierce the bay leaf onto the onion. Place the studded onion into a small pot and cover with the milk.

2. Slowly bring the milk up to a simmer; as soon as the milk is simmering turn off the heat and allow the studded onion to flavour the milk.

3. Melt the butter in another small pan then add the flour and mix to form a thick paste called a roux.

4. Cook out for 3 to 4 minutes then slowly start to add the warm, flavoured milk. Stir continuously while you add the milk until you achieve a smooth sauce with the consistency of thick double cream. If you add the milk a little at a time you will avoid making a lumpy sauce.

5. Cook this out for 10 minutes over a very low heat to avoid burning the sauce, stirring every minute or so.

6. Take off the heat and stir in the cheese (save some Cheddar for the topping), fish, mustard, spring onions, chives, sweetcorn and peas. Spoon into an ovenproof dish.

7. Spoon or pipe the mashed potato on top and sprinkle with Cheddar cheese.

8. Place into the oven, preheated to 200°C, for 20 to 25 minutes or until golden and bubbling at the edges.

46. Pan fried pork loin steak with mixed bean, chorizo and baby spinach stew

4 pork loin steaks

1 Chorizo Rosario, sliced

2 red onions, diced

3 cloves of garlic, crushed

1 tin of mixed beans, drained and rinsed

2 tsp Cajun spice

3 plum tomatoes, diced

100ml hot water

25g tomato purée

1 tbsp white wine vinegar

1/4 pack of baby spinach

Oil for cooking and marinating

Salt, pepper and sugar, to taste

This recipe is best started the day before so you can allow the pork steak plenty of time to marinate in the Cajun spice. In the final stages of cooking, be sure to taste and taste again to get the balance of the sauce just right.

1. Place your pork loin steaks into a zip-lock bag with a little of the oil and a teaspoon of Cajun spice. Marinate this overnight.

2. When you're ready to make the stew, add a little oil to a heavy-bottomed pan add a little oil and then add the sliced chorizo. Remove the skin from the chorizo before you slice it, as the skin won't cook and be stringy to eat.

3. Cook out the chorizo until you gain some colour and there's some of its beautiful red oil in the pan.

4. Next add the diced red onion, cook for a few minutes, then add the crushed garlic. Always be careful once you have added the garlic as it burns very easily.

5. Now add the tomato purée and diced tomato. Very ripe tomatoes work best as they are packed with flavour and will quickly break down to make the sauce. This will only require a very short time on the stove before you can continue adding the rest of the ingredients.

6. Add a little water, the remaining Cajun spice and a little white wine vinegar to taste. You might need a little sugar to find the balance of the sauce. Bring all this to the boil.

7. Taste, taste, taste – make sure you are happy with the balance and seasoning of the dish.

8. To cook the pork, place a large frying pan on the stove and get it very hot. Add a little oil to the pan and then place the pork steaks into the oil. This should make a nice sizzling sound; if you don't get the sizzle it's not hot enough so remove the steaks and reheat the pan. If it's making loads of noise and ruining your clothes turn it down.

9. Pork steaks should only take a few minutes to cook. Once the steaks are firm to the touch they are ready. Remove them from the pan, place onto a tray and let them rest for a couple of minutes. Resting the meat will allow the juices to settle and help retain moisture in the meat.

10. While the meat is resting you can finish off the stew. Add your spinach and the drained mixed beans. Mix everything together and you should be ready to serve.

47. Chicken baked with Serrano ham,
Manchego cheese, olives and pesto

2 x 400g chopped tinned
  tomatoes

4 sticks of celery,
  chopped small

1 red onion, diced

50g tomato purée

1 tsp chilli flakes

1 pinch of dried mixed
  herbs

1 clove of garlic, crushed

2 chicken breasts

4 slices of Serrano ham,
  halved

8 slices of Manchego
  cheese

1 small jar of mixed olives

1 punnet of cherry
  tomatoes, halved

Quality oil

Salt and pepper, to taste

1 tbsp sugar, to taste

Juice of 1 lemon, to taste

For the pesto

See recipe on page 138,
  if you would like to make
  your own

This dish is based on a delicious combination of simple flavours and makes for a fabulous Sunday evening supper. It's especially nice served with wholegrain mustard on the side.

1. For the sauce heat a heavy-bottomed pan and add a dash of oil.
2. Add the chopped celery and diced red onion and sweat for 5 minutes without colouring.
3. Add the garlic and continue to cook for 1 minute before adding the tinned tomatoes, the tomato purée, chilli flakes and mixed herbs.
4. Stir well and cook slowly for 30 minutes.
5. Preheat the oven to 180°C.
6. Season to taste adding either the lemon juice or the sugar as required.
7. Cut the chicken breasts into about 4 thick slices at an angle.
8. In a frying pan colour the chicken pieces, remove from the pan and then wrap each piece in Serrano ham.
9. Pour a thin layer of tomato sauce into the bottom of your ovenproof dish.
10. Layer the ham-wrapped chicken in the dish on top of the sauce.
11. Place the Manchego cheese on top of the chicken, then pop in the olives and halved cherry tomatoes .
12. Place the dish into the oven and cook for 20 minutes.
13. Once cooked, top with pesto and serve.

48. Roast rump of lamb with crushed potatoes, green vegetables and barley

Plan this great meat-and-two-veg dish ahead if you can – the lamb and barley will benefit from some attention the day before. For the green vegetables buy what's nice – the selection isn't set in stone.

4 x 150g rumps of lamb

600g baby new potatoes

1 bunch of flat parsley, shredded

A few sprigs of rosemary

A few sprigs of thyme

3 cloves of garlic

100g barley, soaked overnight if possible

50g butter

Cooking oil

A pinch of salt

For the green vegetables

100g peas, frozen is fine

1 bunch of asparagus

100g French beans

100g snap peas

1. First, get the potatoes cooked. Baby new potatoes are traditionally cooked in boiling water, but if you cook from cold you get a more even cook. One thing for sure is you need a proper pinch of salt.

2. Pour the cooked potatoes into a colander and let them steam out. Never cool in cold water even if you are cooking the day before. Steaming out lets the potatoes dry out and you get a better result.

3. Now onto the lamb. Rump of lamb is a fantastic cut: full of flavour and texture. I would always recommend marinating the rump with a little oil and chopped rosemary and garlic, the longer the better.

4. Now onto the green vegetables. You will need to blanch and refresh them – see page 9 for how to do this.

5. If you've had chance to soak it, the barley will cook very quickly. But don't worry if not. Simply give the barley a good rinse under running cold water, pop it into a pot with a clove of garlic, a sprig of thyme and rosemary and a pinch of salt, then cover in cold water and bring to the boil. As soon as it starts to boil turn down the heat and let it simmer until cooked.

6. To cook the lamb, preheat the oven to 200°C, then place a frying pan onto the heat. Once hot add a little oil and place your rumps of lamb skin-side down onto the pan. At this stage you need good temperature control. You are trying to render down the fat. This fat is very tasty but unless it's cooked down it's not great to eat. Once you have cooked the fat place a clove of garlic and a sprig of rosemary and thyme in the pan.

7. Turn the meat over and brown all its outer surfaces. Remove the lamb from the pan, top with a little butter and pop into the oven for about 6 to 8 minutes.

8. Meanwhile, get your potatoes into a pot with the remainder of the butter and the shredded parsley. Use your wooden spoon to crush the potatoes down as they warm through.

9. Pop the green vegetables into a pan with a little butter and warm through with the barley.

10. Remove the lamb from the oven and rest; with the cuts being so small the resting time is short but vital.

11. Once the lamb is rested, carve into thin slices cutting through the grain and not with it – that way the meat will be much more tender to eat. If your first cut reveals long strands of muscle then turn it 90 degrees and cut from that point.

12. Double check the seasoning on everything and enjoy.

49. Whole roast chicken

1 whole chicken, high welfare is best

1 onion, roughly chopped

1 carrot, roughly chopped

3 sticks of celery, roughly chopped

1 bulb of garlic, cut in half through the circumference

2 sprigs of thyme

2 sprigs of rosemary

30ml sunflower oil

Salt and cracked black pepper

40 cm butcher's string

A meat thermometer, if you have one

For me, a juicy well-cooked roast chicken is a real crowd pleaser. In this recipe I'm a wee bit less conventional: I'm going to embrace common sense cookery. I'll ask you to cook your chicken upside down; yes, upside down. Normally, gravity draws all the moisture and juices down into the cavity of the bird as it cooks and then we carve the meat off, take the legs off and throw away the carcass that's left with all the flavour in it. So, if you cook the bird upside down the juice and the flavour from the carcass is drawn into the breast meat. Don't worry about missing out on the golden crisp skin: we finish the bird off the right way up to create that lovely golden finish.

1. Preheat your oven to 200°C.

2. Whether you choose a standard chicken, free range or organic is your personal choice, but if possible, go for the best you can afford. A small chicken weighs approximately 1.2kg and will feed 2 to 3 people; a medium chicken weighs 1.75kg and feeds 3 to 4 people; a large chicken weighs 2kg and feeds 4 to 6 people.

3. Once all your vegetables are prepared place them into a deep roasting tray. This will provide a barrier between the hot tray and the chicken, will help any juices not to evaporate, and the vegetables and juices can be used to make your roast gravy (see recipe on page 142).

4. Now to your chicken. You will probably find that your chicken has been trussed with an elastic band. This serves a very important job: it pulls the bird together so the legs are pulled in tight against the lower thinner part of the breast. This helps the bird cook more evenly as the legs protect the breast meat.

5. You need to remove the band for now. Have a look inside the bird's cavity and you might find a little bag of innards. If so, open it up, remove the liver and pop everything else in the tray with the chopped vegetables. You can pan fry the liver separately later.

6. Now get the chicken ready for the oven. With a generous pinch of salt season the inside of the cavity and the outside of the bird. Stuff the cavity with half the bulb of garlic and the herbs. Then rub some oil into the chicken skin.

7. Next replace the elastic band back around the chicken. If you don't have an elastic band, use the butcher's string.

8. Place the bird on the tray breast side down and pop into the oven. The time needed depends on the weight of the bird. The guide is 40 minutes per kilo plus 20 minutes.

continues on the next page

49. Whole roast chicken

9. Calculate your total time in the oven, then cook the chicken upside down for three-quarters of that time. Next carefully turn the bird the right side up and finish the cooking.

10. The chicken must be thoroughly cooked before serving, without any pink meat. Pierce the thickest part of the thigh with a skewer and let the juices run out. If they are clear, then it's cooked, but if they still look pink, return it to the oven for 15 minutes, then test again. If you have a meat thermometer, push the probe into the thickest part of the thigh. The temperature should be 75°C before serving.

11. The next stage is vital: rest the bird before carving. This should be done for at least 15 minutes. Resting allows the meat to settle, and it is much more moist as a result.

12. Now carve the bird. Remove the legs by popping them off their ball and socket joint at the pelvic bone; each leg can be cut into two joints – the thigh and the drum stick – giving four pieces of brown meat.

13. Next use a carving knife to slice the breast meat into thin slices until you reach the carcass. Do this on both sides until you have recovered all the meat.

14. Finally, make sure you keep the remaining carcass as it makes the most amazing roast gravy (see recipe on page 142).

Pan roast chicken with cabbage and bacon

50. Pan roast chicken with cabbage, bacon, dauphinoise potatoes and French beans wrapped in bacon

4 chicken breasts, skin on

1 savoy cabbage

50g wholegrain mustard

12 rashers of dry cured bacon

150g French beans

1 pack of chives, chopped

50g butter, or cooking oil

For the dauphinoise potatoes
See recipe on page 149

This dish is a huge hit in my house. Whenever we ask visitors what they would like for dinner they always ask for this dish. It's super simple and packed with flavour. With the crisp skin of the chicken and the crunchy green vegetables enhanced with bacon, what's not to love?

1. The first thing you will need to have organised is the dauphinoise potatoes, and the good news is this can be done in advance. If you don't have time or are looking for something a bit healthier this dish works well with simple boiled new potatoes.

2. To prepare the cabbage remove the outer leaves, which are normally very dark and sometimes damaged, then discard.

3. Cut the root off and start to remove the leaves until you get to the centre. Take each leaf and remove the centre spine and discard.

4. Shred the leaves by rolling them up tightly and running your knife through them as thinly as you can until all the leaves have been cut.

5. With the centre core, quarter it and shred; there's no need to remove the centre spine as the centre is very tender.

6. Preheat your oven to 200°C.

7. To prepare the French beans cut off the top and tail. Then blanch and refresh the cabbage and the French beans. See page 9 for details of how to do this.

8. In a hot pan, sear your chicken breasts, skin-side down first until crisp and golden. Remove from the pan, place onto a roasting tray and pop into the oven for about 15 minutes.

9. Take a few small bunches of French beans and half of your bacon rashers and tightly wrap the beans in the bacon.

10. Pan fry the wrapped beans until the bacon has cooked through. The beans will remain bright green thanks to the blanching and refreshing process.

11. Once cooked, slice the wrapped beans and bacon into 1 cm slices.

12. Take the other half of your bacon and cut into thin strips. Now pan fry the bacon until cooked, add the blanched cabbage, chopped chives and the wholegrain mustard and mix well.

13. Once the chicken breast is cooked you are ready to serve along with your dauphinoise potatoes.

51. **Braised beef** with mashed potatoes and roasted roots

For the braised beef

4 x 175g beef braising
  steaks

40g flour

1 carrot, chopped

1 celery stick, chopped

1 onion, chopped

2 cloves of garlic, crushed

100ml red wine

2 sprigs of rosemary

4 sprigs of thyme

400ml beef stock or
  brown chicken stock

Salt, to taste

Cooking oil

For the roasted roots

2 carrots, large

2 parsnips

25g butter, optional

20g honey

2 sprigs of thyme

20ml quality oil

This slow-cooked dish yields perfectly tender beef. You can use an oven, but a pressure cooker gives great results. The cooking time is only about 20 to 30 minutes once pressure is established. On a cold evening it's delicious with mashed potato and proper gravy – see recipes on pages 147 and 142.

Braised beef

1. Preheat your oven to 130°C. After that, your first task is to roughly chop the onion, carrot and the celery.
2. Next, dust the beef with flour. This helps protect the meat and will also help thicken the sauce.
3. Place the pan on the stove until hot then add a teaspoon of oil.
4. Place the beef into the hot oil and heat until it's coloured well on all sides, then take it out of the pan.
5. If you need to, add more oil. Then add the chopped vegetables to the pan and again colour slightly.
6. Now add the crushed garlic and the herbs.
7. Next add the wine. This helps lift all the flavour from the pan.
8. Now add the stock and bring to the boil. Turn down the heat, put the beef back in and place in the oven for between 60 and 90 minutes, or until the beef is nice and tender.

Roasted roots

1. Wash, peel and then rewash the carrots and the parsnips.
2. Depending on how big the vegetables are, you might want to halve or even quarter them lengthwise to make them fit in the pan.
3. Place the vegetables into a frying pan with the oil and colour slightly, then add the herbs and the butter (optional), and reduce the heat.
4. Place into the oven until the vegetables are cooked – this will take up to an hour.
5. Remove from the oven and drizzle with honey.

52. Oven baked cannelloni with ricotta, butternut squash and almonds

This meat-free recipe uses butternut squash, which has a gorgeous flavour but can be tricky to peel. Here's how I do it. First, top and tail the squash, then cut it in half to separate the bulbous bit from the long top. Now place the cut end on your cutting board and tack your knife from top to bottom peeling a couple of centimetres off at a time. Then cut the bulbous bit in half lengthwise and remove the seeds. Cut each piece into a manageable size and dice.

For the sauce

300ml double cream

15g butter

2 large shallots, finely diced

100ml dry white wine

100ml vegetable stock, you can use a good quality stock cube

For the ricotta mix

8 lasagne sheets, dried

350g ricotta cheese

1/2 butternut squash, peeled and finely diced

50g Parmesan

50g sliced almonds

1/4 packet of flat parsley, shredded

Quality oil

Butter, a little for cooking

Cocktail sticks

Salt and pepper, to taste

1. Make the sauce first so it's ready for when the ricotta and cannelloni are prepared. Over a medium heat melt the butter and once the butter starts to foam add the finely diced shallots and cook without colour for up to a minute until translucent and softened.

2. Add the white wine, then turn up the heat to bring to a rapid boil and reduce the wine by a half.

3. Add the stock and again rapidly reduce by a half. Now pour in the cream and lower the heat in the pan to a gentle simmer as the cream reduces.

4. The sauce will begin to naturally thicken. Reduce it by about a quarter until the sauce glazes the back of a tablespoon.

5. Now for the next stage. Preheat your oven to 180°C.

6. Cook your diced squash in a pan over a low heat with a little butter until softened, then allow it to cool.

7. Add the cooled butternut squash to the ricotta then add the parsley and Parmesan.

8. To cook the pasta sheets, bring a large pot of salted water with a little oil in to the boil and add the sheets. Once they are cooked carefully remove them, dry off any excess water and brush with a little oil.

9. To assemble the cannellonis, place the ricotta mix at the end of the pasta sheet and roll up to form a tight cigar shape.

10. Cut each pasta roll into four equal parts, using a cocktail stick to hold each roll together.

11. Put them cut end up into in an ovenproof dish and spoon over the sauce. Bake for 10 minutes or until piping hot. Sprinkle over almonds and serve straight away.

NICE AND SLOW

I just love braised and slow-cooked food; for one, it uses cheaper cuts, and the cheaper cuts have loads more flavour than the prime cuts. The muscles have been worked hard in the animal: this creates toughness in cuts that require a little more thought on how to cook them, but it also develops flavour and gives you a much more interesting dish. When cooking the tougher cuts, you need to be good at forward planning, as these dishes take time to cook. You will need to enlist a good butcher because you might struggle to find pig's cheeks and ox tail in your local supermarket, but both of these are brilliant and worth hunting down.

Your options on how to cook these cuts are many. If it's a wet dish – i.e. cooked in liquid – then you can pop the food into a casserole dish or a pot and bake in the oven long and slow at around 130°C. Your other option is to cook on the stove in a pot with a lid. I'm not so keen on this method as it takes work to ensure the food won't burn or stick. The other option is a slow cooker. I understand that they are very convenient, but when I had one I felt it sucked the life out of food and gave everything a similar texture and flavour.

My preferred method of cooking long and slow is to use a pressure cooker. Funnily enough, it's not a slow method at all. I started using pressure cookers about ten years ago for culinary competitions. To be truthful, I was terrified. All I had as a reference point was the one my mum used in the 1970s, a hissing scary thing as I remember. Things have moved on since then – and now they are brilliant at home; I have two that I use every week. For me, anything that comes out of the pressure cooker is amazing: it can capture and hold flavours like a dream. I am a big fan!

53. Belly of pork with set polenta, black pudding, spinach and apricots

For the pork

1kg pork belly, rind removed

1 onion, roughly chopped

1 carrot, peeled and chopped

1/2 pack of thyme, picked

2 cloves of garlic, chopped

30ml quality oil

1 tsp paprika

1/2 tsp chilli powder

1/2 tsp ground cumin

150ml vegetable stock, a cube is ideal

Salt, to season

For the set polenta

1.5 litres of vegetable stock, a quality cube will work

350g polenta

75g Parmesan, grated

Salt, to taste

Quality oil, to finish

For the black pudding

150g black pudding, diced

100g dried apricots, sliced

1/2 packet of baby spinach, stalks removed

Belly is a fantastic flavoursome cut of pork. The recipe will take some planning, as it needs to be done over two days, but once you have tasted it I'm sure you will agree that all the hard work is worth it. Before you know it, you'll be cooking belly of pork all the time!

Pork

1. Preheat your oven to 130°C.
2. Take the pork belly and rub in the oil. Next, gradually rub in the spices and a little salt.
3. Place your cut vegetables, garlic and herbs into a deep roasting tray, pop the pork onto the top of them then pour in the vegetable stock.
4. Now cover the tray with a couple of sheets of tinfoil and bake in the oven for 2 to 2.5 hours depending on the pork.
5. Once cooked, carefully remove the pork from the tray and place into another tray. Then place a clean tray on top of the hot pork and, with a couple of cans, press the belly until cold.
6. Once cold the pork can be cut and reheated when needed.

Set polenta

1. Bring 1.5 litres of vegetable stock to the boil in a large pan.
2. Once boiling, gradually start to add the polenta, stirring it in continually with a wooden spoon.
3. Once you have added all the polenta lower the heat so it isn't spluttering too much, then cook, stirring occasionally, for 10 minutes.
4. Meanwhile, line a 20 x 30 cm tray with baking parchment.
5. Now stir the Parmesan into the polenta, check the seasoning and then spoon out onto the tray.
6. Cover with another sheet of baking parchment and a flat baking tray, then top with some cans to press and flatten the polenta. Allow to cool before placing into the fridge.
7. Once cold cut into triangles, brush with a little oil and griddle when needed.

Apricot and black pudding

1. In a large hot frying pan add your diced black pudding and cook until it has started to crisp up.
2. Add the apricots and cook for a couple of minutes.
3. Lastly add the spinach and cook until the spinach has wilted.
4. Double check the seasoning and serve when ready.

54. Braised pig's cheeks with mashed potatoes, red cabbage and pear

1kg pig's cheeks

100g flour, for dusting the pork, optional

1 carrot, peeled and roughly chopped

1 stick of celery, peeled and roughly chopped

1 medium onion, chopped

2 sprigs of thyme

2 cloves of garlic, chopped

50g tomato purée

2 litres of beef stock, or brown stock if you prefer

Cooking oil

Salt and pepper, to taste

For the red cabbage

1/2 red cabbage, shredded

2 banana shallots, chopped

50g sultanas

30ml red wine vinegar

50g brown sugar

1/2 tsp allspice

Pinch of ground ginger

1 Williams pear, chopped

For the mashed potatoes
See recipe on page 147

Pig's cheeks – I love them! Perhaps they don't sound particularly appetising, but for me they are one amazing cut of pork. Before you start you might have to spend a little time trimming them. I always try and get the butcher to trim them for me.

1. The first task is to get the pig's cheeks cooking. I always cook them in a pressure cooker, but if you don't have one you will need to preheat your oven to 130°C.

2. Put your pot onto the stove, add a little oil, roll your pig's cheeks in a little flour and pop them into the hot pot.

3. Do this one at a time until the bottom of the pot is covered. You might need to do this in a couple of batches. It is vital at this stage that you create a lot of colour on the pork – this colour will transfer itself into big flavour.

4. Once all the pork is browned add the chopped onion, celery, carrot, thyme and garlic.

5. Give it a good mix, then once the vegetables have started to soften add the tomato purée and the stock and bring to the boil. You might have to add a little water depending of the size of your pressure cooker.

6. Pop on the lid and bring up to pressure. Once you have established pressure turn the heat down to as low as it will go and cook for 45 minutes. If you haven't got a pressure cooker you can pop the mix into a deep tray, cover with tinfoil and braise in the oven for about 2.5 hours.

7. Next, place the shredded red cabbage, spices, chopped shallots vinegar and sugar into a large pot. Slowly cook with the lid on until the cabbage is tender.

8. Next add the sultanas and the chopped pear and cook for another 10 minutes.

9. Once the pork is ready pass the cooking liquid into a pot and bring to the boil on the stove. Reduce until you have a tasty sauce.

10. Once your sauce is ready pop the cheeks back in.

11. When the cheeks are hot, serve with the mashed potato and the red cabbage.

55. Braised oxtail with vegetables, butter beans and baby onions

Oxtail might not be in your shopping basket every week, but if you've never tried it before then give it a go. I love everything about this cut: the flavour is incredible, and the texture is really different. Here's a perfect winter's night tea – it's a one-pot wonder, especially if you have a pressure cooker as it can all be prepared in thirty minutes and cooked in forty-five.

1 oxtail, cut through the joints, 1kg to 1.5kg

2 carrots, peeled and chopped into 2 cm dice

1/2 savoy cabbage, shredded

2 sticks of celery, peeled and chopped into 2 cm dice

1/2 head of celeriac, peeled and chopped into 2 cm dice

100g baby onions, peeled

100g mushrooms, quartered

2 litres of beef stock, or brown stock if you prefer

25g tomato purée

1/2 bulb of garlic, chopped

175ml red wine

25g plain flour

2 sprigs of rosemary

2 sprigs of thyme

1 tin of butter beans, drained and rinsed

Cracked black pepper, to season

1. If you don't have a pressure cooker, then preheat your oven to 200°C.

2. The first thing to do is to get all your vegetables prepared. The size and shape won't really matter, but keep the cabbage separate at this stage.

3. The next job is to brown the oxtail. You can do this one of two ways: in the pot you are using or in a tray in an oven set to 200°C. Once done, reduce the oven to 150°C if you need it to cook your oxtail.

4. Once you have browned the oxtail, remove it from the pan and add the carrots, celery, baby onions, mushrooms and celeriac. Soften the vegetables, next add the garlic and cook for two minutes.

5. Follow with the tomato purée and the flour.

6. This should all start getting a little sticky at this stage, which means it's now time to add the red wine.

7. Cook until all the wine has been incorporated into the vegetables.

8. Add the stock and the herbs.

9. Put the browned oxtail in, pop the lid on the pressure cooker and bring up to pressure. Once it is pressurised reduce the temperature and cook for about 50 minutes. If you don't have a pressure cooker cook in a tray or large casserole dish in the oven for about 2.5 hours at 150°C.

10. Once the meat is falling off the bone remove all the oxtail onto a tray and allow to cook until you can handle it. You will find that the oxtail muscle is made up of little round nuggets of meat that will just pop out leaving the bone and fat behind.

11. Put all those little nuggets of meat back into the pot.

12. Next add the shredded savoy cabbage and the butter beans and bring to the boil.

13. Reduce the heat then double check the seasoning. I think a good few turns of cracked black pepper work amazingly well with this dish.

56. Lager braised lamb with ratatouille and polenta fries

For the lamb

600g neck of lamb fillet, cut into large chunks

2 white onions, sliced

1/2 carrot, peeled and chopped

1/2 white of leek, washed and chopped

2 sticks of celery, peeled and chopped

1 bottle of Italian lager

1/2 tsp of garlic, chopped

1 tsp of fennel seeds

1 bay leaf

1 litre of beef stock, or brown stock if you prefer

Sprinkle of plain flour

For the ratatouille

300g ripe fresh tomatoes, roughly chopped

1 red onion, cut into 2 cm cubes

1 red pepper, deseeded and cut into 2 cm cubes

1 aubergine, cut into 2 cm cubes

2 courgettes, cut into 2 cm cubes

2 tbsp quality oil, plus some for drizzling

3 garlic cloves, chopped

1/2 bunch of oregano, picked and shredded

1/2 bunch of flat leaf parsley, shredded

1/2 tsp of dried oregano

Salt, pepper and sugar, to taste

For the polenta fries

See recipe on page 150

I have been cooking this recipe for years. I first saw it on a travel food show, tried it and loved the results. I use a neck of lamb fillet – it's an incredible cut which has got the balance of fat to meat just right – but you can try with shoulder if you prefer.

Lamb

1. First, preheat the oven to 160°C.
2. Then put the carrot, leek, celery and lamb into a deep casserole dish.
3. Add the chopped garlic, bay leaf and fennel seeds, top with the lager and a little stock – just enough to cover the ingredients.
4. Cover with a tight fitting lid and pop into the oven for about 1.5 to 2 hours.
5. Remove from the oven when tender. Take the cooked lamb out of the tray and put to one side. Pass the cooking liquid into a jug and put to one side.
6. In a large pan slowly caramelise your sliced onions.
7. Once you have a bit of colour, dust with a little flour.
8. Next add the remainder of your stock and the cooking liquid from the lamb. Reduce this until you get the right flavour and consistency. Once it is tasting good, pop the lamb back in the tray with the sauce until you need it.

Ratatouille

1. Pour the oil into a large pan, then when it is hot add the diced aubergine, courgettes, pepper and chopped onion.
2. Cook for about 5 minutes then add the chopped garlic and the dried oregano.
3. Next add the chopped tomatoes and the fresh shredded oregano.
4. Turn down the heat, pop on a lid and cook the ratatouille out for about 20 minutes.
5. Taste and adjust the seasoning. It might need a little sugar for balance depending on the tomatoes.

Polenta fries

1. Make them according to the recipe on page 150.

57. Lamb shank with beans and sundried tomatoes

4 lamb shanks

1 tin of borlotti beans, drained and rinsed

1 tin of mixed beans, drained and rinsed

2 tins of chopped tomatoes

75g sundried tomatoes, sliced

50g tomato purée

25g plain flour

2 sticks of celery, peeled and diced

1/2 bulb of garlic, chopped

1 large onion, diced

100ml red wine

200ml chicken stock, a quality cube works well

1/2 bunch of flat parsley, shredded

4 sprigs of rosemary

1 bunch of spring onions, sliced

25ml quality oil

Lamb shank is a great cut of meat, which becomes deliciously tender when cooked slowly. Everyone seems to enjoy how each piece makes an individual portion.

1. Preheat your oven to 160°C.

2. The first task is to prepare the vegetables, drain and rinse the beans, slice down the sundried tomatoes.

3. Pop your lamb shanks onto a large roasting tray, drizzle with oil and put on the top of the stove to brown. Make sure you keep the lamb turning to achieve a good colour all over.

4. Remove the lamb and add the onion, celery and rosemary to the heat.

5. Next add the garlic, tomato purée and a little dusting of flour.

6. Mix well, add the tinned tomato, wine and chicken stock, bring to the boil and add the lamb back in. Ideally you have enough liquid to cover the lamb.

7. Next cover with a double layer of tinfoil and pop into the oven. Cook for about 1.5 to 2 hours until the lamb is nice and tender.

8. Once the lamb is cooked remove from the tray and add the beans, flat parsley, spring onions and sundried tomatoes. Now bring to the boil on the stove top.

9. Double check the consistency and the seasoning. Depending on the tomato it might need a little sugar to balance it out.

10. Add the lamb back into the sauce mixture to heat up.

11. Once hot serve with some focaccia bread – see recipe on page 157.

ON THE SIDE

The much-neglected elements of a great plate of food are all in this chapter. We pay so much attention to the main part of a dish, but I feel if you get the side stuff right it can make all the difference to the perfect plate of food. Here, I have bunched all the 'problem children' into the one spot. That's because I find people struggle with things like proper sauces, rice and potatoes. The reality is once you understand the rules for each of these elements it's very simple to get them right and the joy of it is that they will really elevate your skills in the kitchen. You'll see that I have also popped a couple of bread recipes in. Bread is brilliantly easy and brilliantly therapeutic to make. There is nothing better than taking some very simple ingredients and transforming them into something amazing. Watch out: once you start making your own bread it becomes addictive.

7

58. Pesto

1 bunch of basil
50g Parmesan
50g pine nuts
2 cloves of garlic
50ml quality oil
Salt, to taste

I love homemade pesto. It is by far one of the easiest sauces to make and is a million times tastier than what you get out of a jar. Always make sure you taste, as seasoning with pesto is vital. It's a very adaptable recipe – you can substitute pine nuts for any other nut and you can omit the garlic if you like a more herby flavour. Remember not to store fresh basil in the fridge: it hates the cold and will go black.

1. Place all the ingredients into the blender or food processer and blitz down. Try not to blitz for too long as it will heat up the sauce and discolour the basil.

2. Pesto will keep very well in a sealed jar in the fridge, but make sure you add a little extra oil to it once it's in the jar.

59. Gremolata

1 bunch of flat leaf parsley
2 cloves of garlic
1 lemon, zested

Gremolata is a gorgeously zesty Italian herb sauce, which also makes for a delicious marinade.

1. The first thing to do is to wash your flat leaf parsley.

2. Once washed make sure you dry it. Kitchen paper works well or, if you have one, a salad spinner is great.

3. Next pick the parsley leaves from the stalks.

4. Gremolata is better when the parsley is hand chopped. To do this take a small bunch of picked parsley leaves and roll them up nice and tight. Then, with a cook's knife, shred the leaves very, very finely and repeat until all the parsley is chopped.

5. Next peel, crush and chop the garlic and add to the parsley.

6. Add the lemon zest and continue to chop until the parsley, garlic and lemon are well combined.

7. It's best to use gremolata on the day you make it, but you can store it in the fridge for a couple of days.

60. Simple tomato sauce

2 x 400g tins of chopped tomatoes
50g tomato purée
2 sticks of celery
1/2 onion
1 carrot
1/2 red chilli
Pinch of oregano, dried
1 clove of garlic
1 tsp plain flour
1 tsp sugar, to taste
1 tsp vinegar
Quality oil
Salt and freshly cracked black pepper

In my opinion, the way to make the best-tasting tomato sauce is to follow four simple rules.

- Chop the vegetables down as finely as you can.
- Don't cook the sauce too long.
- Don't blitz or purée the sauce.
- Use plenty of celery. It adds an amazing flavour, so the more the better.

1. First prepare all the vegetables. You will need to peel the celery – yes, I said peel the celery! To do this take your peeler from the top to the bottom of the celery stick and remove the horrible stringy bits. Now cut into manageable lengths, then into thin strips and lastly dice.

2. Next chop the onion, garlic and chilli.

3. Lastly dice the carrot as finely as you can.

4. You are now ready to cook. Take a heavy-bottomed pan then add a little oil. Once you have gained some heat add the onion, celery and carrot.

5. Cook for a few minutes without colour. The vegetables should start to look sticky, but control the heat to ensure you don't burn them.

6. Next add the chopped garlic, chilli, a pinch of oregano and cook for a couple of minutes.

7. Then add the tomato purée and cook for two more minutes.

8. Next add the teaspoon of flour. I find that flour helps hold the sauce together, but it's optional.

9. Once the flour has been worked in add the tinned tomatoes.

10. Bring to the boil, pop on a lid and then reduce the heat as low as it will go for about 20 minutes.

11. Once cooked give it a taste. You will find it might need some work to get the balance right so add the vinegar and the sugar, then some seasoning.

12. Once you are happy with the flavour you have two choices. You can either use the sauce as it is or, if you would like a smoother finish, pass the sauce through a sieve. This will ensure that the sauce keeps its amazing red colour.

61. Salsa verde

2 or 3 cloves of garlic
6 anchovy fillets
2 banana shallots
1 lemon, zested
4 tbsp capers
1 tsp Dijon mustard
1 bunch of flat parsley
1 bunch of mint
1 bunch of basil
Quality oil

This is a very easy recipe to pull together. To make it truly authentic and full of flavour, take your time to chop all the herbs by hand.

1. The first job is to finely chop the garlic and the shallots.
2. Next wash and dry all the herbs, then chop them with a cook's knife.
3. Now cut the capers in half.
4. Chop down the anchovies.
5. You are now ready to bring it together. Add the mustard, lemon zest and all your chopped ingredients into a bowl and mix together.
6. Gradually add the olive oil until it forms a paste.
7. Taste and adjust the seasoning.

62. Mayonnaise

2 egg yolks, pasteurised
1 tsp English or Dijon mustard
2 tsp white wine vinegar
200ml quality oil
Salt and ground white pepper

When mayonnaise is made in restaurant kitchens we always use pasteurised egg; even the freshest eggs have a chance of containing the salmonella bug. This recipe can be done by hand using a whisk or in a food processor, but the rules are the same. Mayonnaise is hugely versatile so you can easily add other ingredients to make many other sauces.

1. Place the egg yolks into the food processor or bowl first, next add the mustard and the white wine vinegar. Mix this until all ingredients have combined.
2. Next slowly add the oil. Be very careful at the start of this stage – you'll almost be adding the oil a drop at a time.
3. Once you have added a third of the oil you can add it a little quicker, and after the next third a little quicker again until it's all used up.
4. Don't worry if you split the sauce by adding the oil too fast. Don't throw it away – all you need to do is start off with a fresh egg yolk in a clean bowl and, using the split mixture as you used the oil, it will come back together and form perfect mayonnaise.
5. If the sauce is a little thick you can add some water. Next season to taste. The mix might also be able to take some more vinegar depending on your taste.

63. Béchamel (aka white sauce)

25g butter
25g plain flour
250ml milk
1 bay leaf
2 cloves
1 small onion

Béchamel sauce, made from a white roux and milk, has long been considered one of the key sauces in French cuisine. It's a great sauce to master as you can use it as the base for other sauces.

1. The first job is to peel your onion. Then, using the cloves, pierce the bay leaf onto the onion. Place the studded onion into a small pot and cover with the milk.

2. Slowly bring the milk up to a simmer. As soon as the milk is simmering turn off the heat and allow the studded onion to flavour the milk.

3. Melt the butter in another small pan then add flour and mix to form a roux.

4. Cook out for 3 to 4 minutes then slowly start to add the warm, flavoured milk.

5. Stir continuously while you add the milk until you achieve a smooth sauce with the consistency of thick double cream. If you add the milk a little at a time you will avoid making a lumpy sauce.

6. Cook this out for 10 minutes over a very low heat to avoid burning the sauce, stirring every minute or so.

7. Once cooked cover with cling film or parchment paper to avoid it forming a skin.

64. Proper roast gravy

1 tray of natural juices and stuck bits from your roast lamb, chicken or beef

1 glass of red wine

2 tbsp plain flour

25g tomato purée

1.5 litres of beef stock, the ones in little pouches work well for this

1 carrot, peeled and roughly chopped

1 onion, peeled and roughly chopped

2 sticks of celery, roughly chopped

3 cloves of garlic

2 sprigs of thyme

2 sprigs of rosemary

Gravy is an amazing sauce. For me, it's the real essence of home cooking – nothing fancy and it doesn't involve half a day's work.

1. Start by getting your roasting tray onto the heat on your stove top; then add the chopped vegetables and herbs.

2. You are looking to caramelise the vegetables and lift the flavour off the bottom of the roasting tray. The aim is to make use of what was left from your roast.

3. Next add the garlic and about half of the wine; use the wine to help unstick what's at the bottom of the tray.

4. Next add the tomato purée, mix it in, then add the flour and work it into the mixture. This might start to clump together but don't worry.

5. Add the rest of the wine and bring the whole lot to the boil.

6. Lastly add the stock and whisk it all together.

7. Transfer the mixture into a thick-bottomed pan and reduce over a medium heat until you have the required flavour.

8. The more you reduce your gravy the stronger its flavour will be and the thicker it will become

65. Hollandaise sauce

200g butter

4 egg yolks

50ml white wine vinegar

3 whole black
   peppercorns

1/2 elephant shallot,
   finely diced

Salt, to season

A little lemon juice

Once you understand the science of it, hollandaise isn't difficult to make. But, as the backbone of the classic French repertoire, it has a certain *je ne sais quoi* about it. Forget the hype; it's simply a sauce made of hot egg and butter – be confident and a little cautious and you'll soon have a hollandaise that's curdle free.

1. To start, clarify the butter. To do this, place the butter into a pan and gently heat. You will notice that the butter separates and the milky whey sinks to the bottom of the pan and the clear fat lies on top.

2. Try not to disturb the pan too much by shaking or stirring, then remove from the heat and allow to settle for 2 to 3 minutes.

3. Meanwhile place the vinegar, diced shallot and peppercorns into a separate pan with a splash of cold water and bring to a boil, reducing by a quarter.

4. Once the butter has settled, take a ladle and start to carefully ladle off the clarified butter from the pan into a pouring jug trying not to disturb the whey at the bottom of the pan.

5. Pass the vinegar reduction through a fine sieve to remove the peppercorns and shallots.

6. Place the egg yolks into a steel bowl. Place the bowl over a pot of simmering water. Make sure the bowl doesn't get too hot, as this will overcook the eggs and split the mixture.

7. Slowly add the reduction to the egg yolks, whisking the whole time.

8. Gradually add the melted butter, whisking again the whole time.

9. You need to be very careful at the early stages of adding the melted butter. Just add a tiny amount at a time.

10. As it starts to thicken, you can gradually add more each time. Slowly drizzle the melted butter until all the butter is used. If the sauce is too thick add a teaspoon of water to thin it down to the desired texture.

11. Taste and season with salt and a little squeeze of lemon juice. Serve while the sauce is still warm.

66. Twice-cooked hand-cut chips

Chips are probably the most demonised food on the planet, but done well they are an incredible treat. The most important thing when making your own chips is to select the correct potatoes. I like Red Rooster but King Edwards, Maris Piper, Romano or Desirée will all make a fabulous chip. How thick you cut the potatoes is up to you, but if you go bigger than 2 cm you will need to cook a little longer. The chunkier the chip the less fat you eat, but remember that 'healthier' doesn't mean 'healthy'. If you use a pan to cook your chips, please be careful: oil heats up quicker than you think and can catch fire very easily.

1kg potatoes
1 litre of cooking oil
Sea salt, to season

1. The first job is to scrub the potatoes. I much prefer to keep the skin on, but if you don't fancy eating the skin then peel them.

2. Next cut the potatoes into 2 cm slices then slice these into chips that are 2 cm wide.

3. Place the chips into a pan and rinse under cold running water.

4. Strain, give the pan a rinse and pop the potatoes back into the pan and top up with cold water.

5. Slowly bring to the boil and gently simmer for 3 to 4 minutes. You are looking for the chips to be cooked.

6. Strain through a colander and allow to steam out.

7. Once at room temperature you will find that most of the excess water will be gone. Dry any remaining water with kitchen paper.

8. Keep covered and at room temperature until needed.

9. Heat the oil to 185°C in a deep fat fryer or a large, deep saucepan and cook the chips until golden and crisp. This will take about 5 to 8 minutes. Serve immediately.

67. Perfect roast potatoes

I love roast potatoes. As part of a Sunday roast they are a must, almost as important as the roast itself. You will need a couple of things to make the potatoes exceptional. One is duck fat; I think it makes a huge difference. You will also need a very good potato. I love Red Roosters, but the same potatoes that are perfect for chips are also spot on for roasters.

1kg potatoes
100g duck fat
1 tsp semolina
3 sprigs of rosemary
Sea salt

1. To get started preheat your oven to 210°C, and then peel and cut your potatoes into even sizes.

2. Rinse under running water to remove excess starch.

3. Once rinsed, place into a pot of cold water and a good pinch of salt. Slowly bring to the boil. Once boiling, turn the heat down to a simmer.

4. Simmer the potatoes until a small knife passes easily through them.

5. Drain over a colander and allow to steam out. Every now and again give the potatoes a flip in the colander; this will help them dry out.

6. Ideally you are looking for potatoes that are starting to ever so slightly break up and become rough around the edges. This gives you great crispy edges.

7. Spoon your duck fat into a large roasting tin and place the tray into the hot oven.

8. Once hot carefully pour in your potatoes, then put the tray back into the oven.

9. Every now and again give the potatoes a stir.

10. Once they start to colour you can then add the rosemary and a sprinkle of the semolina and a pinch of sea salt. The semolina will add that little extra crunch.

11. Keep the potatoes in the oven giving them a stir every 5 minutes or so. Once the potatoes are rich and golden, remove from the tray with a slotted spoon onto absorbent paper.

12. You are now ready to serve.

68. Sauté potatoes with onions

1kg baby new potatoes

2 onions

25g butter

1/4 bunch of flat parsley, shredded

Cooking oil

Sea salt

This is super simple to do and a real favourite in my house. The secret is to use two pans: one to sauté the potatoes and one for the onions. Because they are technically both cooked very differently, this enables you to get both elements right.

1. The first job is to cook your new potatoes. Place your potatoes into a large pan of boiling salted water.

2. Meanwhile, slice your onions as thinly as you can. Avoid cutting them into rainbow shapes, as this shape will break down when cooked. Instead turn your onion the other way and follow the lines in the onion to give you a more consistent size and shape of onion.

3. Once your potatoes are cooked, drain them through a colander and allow to steam out. This helps dry out the potatoes and makes for a much better sauté.

4. Once cold, slice the potatoes into 2 cm slices.

5. Put two frying pans onto the stove. Pop a little oil into both, add the onions straight away – there's no need for too much heat.

6. Once the other pan is hot add the potatoes. Only add enough potatoes to cover the bottom; you will probably have to do this in batches.

7. Keep the onions going on a slow, low heat. You are trying to get rid of moisture from the onion – if the pan is too hot the onions caramelise very quickly and you don't get the same deep flavour.

8. Once the potatoes are done and the onions are wonderfully slowly caramelised, mix both together with the shredded parsley and a little bit of butter.

9. Check the seasoning, and serve.

69. Perfect mash

1kg Maris Piper potatoes,
   peeled and cut into large
   even-sized pieces
50g butter
1 egg yolk

Mash – so simple, you need to get it 100% right. A potato ricer or a Mouli grater are amazing tools to help create the perfect mash. My top tip is that when you cook potatoes for mash it's very important to keep the chunks quite large and even. If you cut the potatoes up too small they break up and create loads of starch, which will give you a rubbish mash!

1. In a large pan cover your cut potatoes in cold water, add a good pinch of salt.
2. Slowly bring to the boil. Once the potatoes come to the boil turn the heat down so the water is on simmer.
3. You need to cook the potatoes until you can insert a small knife easily into the potato. Once cooked pass the potatoes through a colander.
4. Allow the potatoes to steam out in the colander. This will get rid of loads of water.
5. After a few minutes return the potatoes to a dry pan and dry out on the stove with a low heat under them.
6. Next you are ready to mash. A potato ricer, a Mouli grater or an old-fashioned potato masher will all get the job done. What's important is that the potato must be mashed while it's still hot.
7. Next put your potato into a large bowl, add the egg yolk and butter and beat until smooth.
8. You are now ready to use either as a side or in loads of different recipes.

70. Fondant potatoes

4 potatoes, such as Maris Piper

50ml vegetable oil

50g butter

1/4 bunch of thyme

2 cloves of garlic, crushed in the skin

200ml chicken stock, a quality cube works well

Salt and pepper, to season

This is a recipe with lots of different stages, but the outcome is wonderful. You will have potatoes rich and tasty with absorbed stock and glorious fluffy centres.

1. Preheat your oven to 200°C.
2. Take a potato and slice off the two largest sides so that you create two flat areas on the potato.
3. Using a plain round pastry cutter, push it into the cut edge of the potato until the cutter completely disappears into the potato.
4. Using a cook's knife cut into the potato and trim around the cutter until you get a perfect cylinder the same shape as the cutter. Push out the potato and repeat for the other potatoes.
5. Place a medium saucepan onto the heat. Make sure the pot can go in the oven: no plastic handles. Pour in the vegetable oil and heat until it sizzles.
6. Place your potato cylinders flat end first into the hot oil. Then lower the heat to medium and cook the potatoes until well browned. This should take 5 to 6 minutes.
7. Flip the potatoes onto the opposite ends. As they cook – for about the same amount of time – use a piece of kitchen roll held with tongs to carefully blot out the oil from the pan.
8. Reduce the heat and add the butter and thyme sprigs to the pan.
9. Next add the crushed garlic. All you need to do is keep the skin on and with the back of your hand crush it against the board.
10. Cook until the butter foams and the foam turns from white to a pale tan colour, then using a spoon baste the butter over the potato.
11. Season with more salt and pepper.
12. Pour the chicken stock into the pan until the potato is covered.
13. Transfer the pan to your preheated oven and cook for 25 to 30 minutes until the potatoes are tender and creamy inside.

71. Dauphinoise potatoes

750g potatoes, peeled and thinly sliced

300g double cream

50g butter

3 cloves of garlic, crushed

1 sprig of thyme

1 sprig of rosemary

100g Gruyère cheese, grated

Salt and pepper

This is a firm favourite in my house. It's not the healthiest of potato dishes but now and again it's a great treat.

1. Preheat the oven to 180°C.
2. In a thick-bottomed pot add the cream, butter, rosemary, thyme and garlic and bring to a boil.
3. Season with salt and pepper.
4. Once the cream solution has boiled, strain and then add the sliced potatoes and slowly simmer until the cream starts to thicken.
5. This thickening is the starch coming out of the potatoes as they start to cook. It also helps speed up the cooking process in the oven.
6. Next carefully layer the potatoes into your tray. I like to add a little grated Gruyère cheese into each layer as I go, while making sure I reserve some for the top at the end.
7. Scatter the top layer with cheese, cover your tray with tinfoil and place into the oven.
8. Bake in the oven at 180°C for 20 minutes and then remove the tinfoil and bake for a further 15 to 20 minutes or until you can easily insert a knife into the potato mix.

72. Spicy sweet potato fries

2 large sweet potatoes
2 tbsp cornflour
75ml cooking oil
1 clove of garlic, chopped
1/2 tsp sea salt flakes
1/2 tsp Cajun spice
1/2 tsp smoked paprika
Black pepper, a few
  turns to season

These make a super-tasty alternative to chips – even the biggest potato devotee will fast become a convert! My top tip is to leave them in the oven as it cools at the end – if you have the patience to do this you'll be rewarded with knockout crispy fries.

1. Preheat the oven to 200°C and line a large baking tray with non-stick parchment paper.
2. Peel and cut the sweet potatoes into thick French fry-style chips.
3. Place your chips into a large sandwich bag or bowl.
4. Mix your salt, pepper, Cajun spice, garlic and paprika with the cornflour. Add this mixture to the cut sweet potatoes and make sure every chip has been covered in this mix. You want a nice thin coating.
5. Pour the potatoes into a colander and shake off any extra mix.
6. Pop the sweet potatoes into a bowl and coat with oil.
7. Place the sweet potatoes onto the baking tray. Try not to overlap or have them touching or else they won't bake, they'll just steam.
8. Bake for 10 minutes. Remove from the oven and flip. Place back into the oven for 15 to 20 minutes more.
9. Turn the oven off and keep the fries inside as the oven cools down for about 30 minutes. This will help the fries get really nice and crisp.

73. Polenta fries

1.5 litres of vegetable
  stock, a cube is fine
350g polenta
75g Parmesan, grated
Cooking oil
Salt, to taste

Starchy corn porridge might be the last thing you'd expect to make chips from. But let go of prejudice and give these superbly crunchy fries a go.

1. Bring your 1.5 litres of vegetable stock to the boil in a large pan.
2. Once boiling gradually start to add the polenta, stirring it in continually with a wooden spoon.
3. Once you have added all the polenta lower the heat so it isn't spluttering too much. Then cook, stirring occasionally, for 10 minutes.
4. Meanwhile, line a 20 x 30 cm tray with baking parchment. Stir the grated Parmesan into the polenta mix, then spoon out onto the tray.
5. Cover with another sheet of baking parchment and a flat baking tray, then top with some cans to press and flatten the polenta. Allow to cool before placing into the fridge.
6. Once cold cut into chips and deep fry in cooking oil at 180°C.
7. Season with salt and serve.

74. Coconut rice

200g Thai jasmine-
  scented white rice
200ml coconut milk
300ml water
1/2 tsp salt
1/2 tsp cooking oil

Coconut rice is the perfect accompaniment to many Thai and Indian dishes, but it's equally fabulous with Western-style food. I use Thai jasmine-scented white rice here; it's easy to find in most supermarkets or, better still, in your local Asian or international store.

1. Rub the oil over the bottom of a deep-sided pot. You will need it to have a tight-fitting lid.
2. Place the rice, coconut milk, water and salt in the pot and set over medium high to high heat. Stir occasionally to keep the rice from sticking to the bottom of the pot and burning.
3. Once the liquid has begun to bubble gently, stop stirring and reduce.
4. Turn off the heat, put on a tight-fitting lid and place in the oven at 140°C until the rice has absorbed most of the liquid. To check, pull the rice aside with a fork to see if most of the liquid is gone.
5. Remove from the oven but leave the covered pot on the burner for another 5 to 10 minutes, or until you're ready to eat.

75. Sticky rice

1 mug glutinous rice
1 mug water
1 stick of lemon grass
A pinch of salt

Why have I moved into American measurements? Don't worry, there's a good reason for this. Rice is often best cooked as a volume recipe rather than weighed. I use a regular coffee mug, which is a great measure for four people. Plan this in advance – your first job is to soak the rice overnight: glutinous rice has a hard outer layer that needs to be softened before cooking.

1. Soak your rice overnight. Once this is done, you're ready to start.
2. Bash the lemon grass with the back of a knife as this help release flavour.
3. Then place the rice into a pot with a tight-fitting lid, add the water and the lemon grass and a pinch of salt.
4. Put the lid on and slowly cook for 15 minutes.
5. Once the rice is cooked, give it a stir and add another tablespoon of water. Stir again with a wooden spoon then place the lid back on for at least 15 minutes.
6. Remove the lemon grass and enjoy.

76. Pilaf rice

1 cup of long grain rice

1.25 cups of stock, a chicken or vegetable stock cube is ideal

1 onion, finely diced

1 bay leaf

20ml cooking oil

This recipe is amazing. It's completely failsafe – and that's because everything is controlled. Measuring the rice and the stock then setting the temperature makes it the same every time. When I refer to a cup I literally just mean a cup or a mug. If you have a lot of people to feed simply use a bigger mug. If you want to check, around 60g to 70g of rice per person is perfect.

1. Use a pan with a tight-fitting lid. Heat the pan and add the oil. Then add the onion and sweat for 4 to 5 minutes without colouring.

2. Add rice and toast for a minute, coating the rice in the oil.

3. Now add the stock and the bay leaf, bring to the boil, then put a tight-fitting lid on the pan.

4. Place in a preheated oven at 170°C for 18 minutes, or until the rice has absorbed all the stock.

5. Allow the rice to stand once it's out of the oven. Then fluff it up with a fork and you're ready to serve.

BREAD

77. Coriander flat breads

350g plain flour

1.5 tsp sugar

1 tsp salt

1/2 tsp baking powder

20g fresh yeast

160g milk

140ml natural yogurt

Bunch of fresh coriander, roughly chopped

Butter for cooking

Different flat breads are cooked all over the world. This foolproof recipe uses yeast and baking powder – many don't – and I love it for its distinctive coriander taste.

1. Sieve all your dry ingredients – but not the yeast – together, then sprinkle in the chopped coriander.

2. I've weighed the milk for this bread, as it's more accurate. In a clean pan, heat the milk, stir in the yogurt, then dissolve in the yeast.

3. Add this mixture to the flour to form a dough. Knead until smooth then cover and leave to prove until doubled in size.

4. Divide the mix into golf ball-sized pieces and roll into the classic teardrop shape.

5. In a warmed non-stick frying pan brush the flat breads with butter and add to the pan. Colour and lightly brush the other side of the bread, then flip over and colour on both sides.

6. Place into a hot oven at 180°C for 4 to 5 minutes.

78. Granary bread

225g white bread flour
225g granary bread flour
10g salt
1 tsp sugar
7g sachet of instant yeast
300g water, warm at 37°C
25g butter

There's nothing quite like making your own bread. The whole process is restorative, calming, pleasingly hard work and I've yet to meet anyone who doesn't love the smell of bread as it bakes and the taste of it fresh from the oven.

1. Sieve the salt and two flours together into a large bowl. You will find that you are left with all the good bits from the granary flour in the sieve. Pop those bits into the mix as well. The main purpose of sieving the flours is to aerate and mix properly.

2. Next measure your water. The best way to get the measurement correct and the temperature of 37°C is to sort the temperature first. In a jug add hot and cold water to get it full of water to baby bottle temperature. The reason you need water at this temperature is that the yeast reacts much quicker at body temperature.

3. Now you can measure the water. I find using scales as opposed to a measuring jug is much more accurate.

4. Now add the yeast and the sugar to the water. The sugar in the mix gives the yeast a real boost and helps activate it a little quicker.

5. Rub the butter into the flours mix.

6. Next make a little well in the centre of the flour and add the water mix. Using a spoon mix the ingredients together until you get a rough dough.

7. Dust your work surface with some flour and then tip the dough out and start to knead the dough. You might have to add a little more flour as you go.

8. Knead the dough until it starts to bounce back when pressed.

9. Place the dough back into your bowl and cover tightly with cling film.

10. The next stage is to allow the dough to rest. You want the dough to double or triple in size, which could take an hour or so depending on how warm your kitchen is.

11. Preheat your oven to 200°C.

12. Once the bread has doubled in size remove it from the bowl and 'knock back'. This is the same as kneading – and once you have knocked out all the air you can shape your bread.

13. You have plenty of options on shape and size. You could use the whole dough to shape into a bloomer, or break it into smaller dinner rolls. You could even bake in a clean ceramic flowerpot. It's entirely up to you.

continues on the next page

78. Granary bread

14. Once you have shaped your dough you now need to prove the bread. This simply means that you cover the shaped bread – with a clean plastic bag or cloth – and leave it to rise before you bake it.

15. The bread should again double in size. Don't be tempted to put the bread in the oven too early, as you will end up with very heavy bread.

16. Cooking times vary with size. Try 45 to 50 minutes for a bloomer and 15 to 20 minutes for small loaves.

17. Once the bread is golden, take it out the oven and let it sit for 5 to 10 minutes. Then take out of the tin and leave to cool on a wire rack.

79. Focaccia bread

450g strong flour
7g sachet of dried yeast
1 tbsp sugar
1 tsp sea salt
300ml warm water
Olive oil, to drizzle
Herbs to season

This is a fantastic bread: it's a very easy introduction to bread making. It was a must-bake dish when I was at the Cook School and it has stayed with me ever since. I love how adaptable it is. You can add any flavours you like. Why not try cherry tomatoes, garlic, hard herbs (rosemary, thyme, parsley), roasted red onions or roasted peppers?

1. Place the flour, salt, sugar and yeast into a bowl and mix well. Now make a well in the centre and add the water.

2. Slowly incorporate the flour and water together until you have a rough dough.

3. Tip out onto work surface and begin to knead. Use enough flour for kneading until you achieve a smooth dough.

4. Place the dough back in the bowl and cover with cling film or a damp cloth. Allow to prove somewhere warm until doubled in size. This takes 30 to 40 minutes.

5. Tip the dough out of the bowl and knead for a minute or two, then mould into the shape of the tray you will bake your bread in.

6. Drizzle with olive oil and a good pinch of Maldon sea salt. You can add any further flavouring you desire.

7. Re-prove your bread for another 15 to 20 minutes or until it has again doubled in size. It should be quicker this time as the yeast has been activated in the first proving.

8. Bake in a preheated oven at 190°C for 18 minutes.

SHOW STOPPERS

I wanted to call this chapter 'Showing Off' because if you are creating any of these dishes, that's what you're doing. This chapter is full of great recipes that provide the wow! factor if you have friends or family over for tea. Some of these recipes have been with me a long time, and I have developed them over many years. Much as they are a bit more complex than what has come before, the skills required are the same. You will just need to put a little more thought into the sourcing of ingredients and your planning of the preparation.

Having said that, there are also some really simple dishes that will require precise cooking to make them stand out. Getting the perfect fish and prime cut cooked to perfection takes a little time to master. Don't be frightened to give any of these recipes a go: just make sure you have everything to hand and ensure you have the very best ingredients.

8

80. Grilled langoustine with fennel, pea and herb salad and aioli

For the fennel salad
1 bulb of fennel

100g peas

1 small bunch of dill, chopped

1 pack of salad cress

1 lemon, peeled, juiced and zested

100ml quality oil

For the aioli
3 egg yolks

4 cloves of garlic

1/2 lemon, juiced

150ml quality oil

For the grilled langoustine
20 langoustines

100g butter, softened

2 cloves of garlic, crushed

1 lemon, zested

Salt

This is actually a beautifully simple dish, but it never fails to impress. It's serious, grown-up food – that's lots of fun to eat too – which makes it ideal for socialising. Little finger bowls with warm water and a lemon slice are a thoughtful addition to the table; langoustines can be messy!

Fennel salad
1. Using a mandolin or a very sharp knife shave thin slices from the bulb of fennel.

2. Using a peeler, peel slices from the skin of the lemon, remove any white pith and cut into thin strips.

3. Make a simple dressing using the juice from the lemon, oil and chopped dill.

4. Mix the salad cress with the fennel, peas and the lemon slices and zest. Then dress lightly with your lemon dressing.

Aioli
1. Place the garlic, lemon juice and egg yolks into a blender and blend all together.

2. Gradually pour the oil into the blender in a steady slow stream, until it forms a thick sauce. The mixture, once blended, should be a thick yellow sauce; if it becomes too thick you can add a little water to thin it down.

Grilled langoustine
1. The first thing you need to do is blanch and refresh the langoustine.

2. Make sure you have a bowl of ice water at the ready to refresh the shellfish once blanched.

3. Now, bring a large pan of water to the boil and add a generous amount of salt to the water; I'd suggest about 15g per litre of water. Plunge the langoustines into the boiling water for 40 seconds, then remove and refresh in the ice water.

4. Once blanched, carefully cut each langoustine in half lengthways. To do this look for a little cross on the top of the langoustine and then, with a large cook's knife, place the point of the knife into the centre of the cross and push down to cut through the body and the tail. Next remove the knife, give it a clean and then finish the job by cutting through the head.

continues on the next page

80. Grilled langoustine with fennel, pea and herb salad and aioli

5. Once halved you will notice a brown sac at the head of the langoustine. Carefully remove this. You will also notice the waste track running through the tail, which you will also need to remove.

6. Repeat with all the langoustines.

7. To make the lemon garlic butter, crush the garlic, zest the lemon and beat in with the softened butter.

8. Next preheat your grill to medium/high.

9. Lay the langoustines cut-side-up on a large roasting tray, loosen them within their shells, and spoon over the lemon garlic butter.

10. Place under the grill for 3 to 4 minutes, or until the butter is bubbling and the langoustines are golden in colour. Be very careful not to overcook.

11. Serve with your fennel salad and aioli.

Pan seared sea bass with mussel and saffron broth

81. Pan seared sea bass with mussel, potato, spinach and saffron broth

4 fillets of sea bass

1kg mussels

1 shallot, finely diced

1 clove of garlic, finely sliced

250ml white wine

1 tomato, blanched, skinned and deseeded

50g peas, frozen

1/2 courgette, diced into 1 cm pieces

2 potatoes, diced into 1 cm pieces

Pinch of saffron

1/2 pack of baby spinach

1 tsp flat parsley, chopped

100ml vegetable stock, a cube is fine for this

50ml double cream

20g butter

1 tsp cooking oil

Salt and pepper, to season

Sea bass is deliciously versatile – its succulent flesh makes it ideal for pan searing and it's the perfect complement to the delicate flavours and textures of the broth.

1. Warm your sauté pan, add a knob of butter and then sweat off half of the shallot and garlic for 2 to 3 minutes.

2. Now add the wine, bring to a boil then add the mussels. Place the lid on and steam for 3 to 4 minutes or until all the shells have opened; if there are any that don't open then discard these.

3. Strain through a sieve, while making sure to keep the liquid, as this will form the base to the broth.

4. Remove meat from the mussel shells and discard the shells.

5. Wipe out the pan, add a knob of butter and add the other half of the shallot. Sweat this for 2 to 3 minutes, then add the cooking liquor and reduce by half.

6. Next add the vegetable stock and reduce by two-thirds, then add the cream and again reduce by a third.

7. Add the diced potatoes and saffron and boil for a few minutes.

8. Once the potatoes have cooked, add the peas, courgettes, spinach and tomato and warm these through.

9. In a non-stick pan heat a teaspoon of oil then add the sea bass skin-side down. Cook for 2 to 3 minutes until the skin is crispy. Turn the fish over, add a knob of butter, take the pan off the heat and allow any residual heat from the pan to finish the cooking.

10. Finally add the mussels and the chopped parsley to the broth. Taste to check and adjust seasoning, then serve in a large bowl with the sea bass on top.

82. Pan seared breast of duck with spiced and caramelised cauliflower, kale, beetroot and baby fondant potatoes

For the duck

4 duck breasts

2 sprigs of rosemary

2 sprigs of thyme

2 cloves of garlic, crushed

20g cooking oil

100g butter

For the cauliflower

1/2 cauliflower

2 sprigs of rosemary

2 sprigs of thyme

1/2 bulb of garlic

100g butter

1 sheet of silicon paper, cartouche

For the beetroot

2 fresh beetroots

2 sprig of thyme

2 sprig of rosemary

50g butter

For the potatoes

2 or 3 large potatoes, Rooster or Maris Piper

35g butter

75ml stock, a chicken or vegetable stock cube works well

Many people think that pan searing duck is a tricky skill to learn, but it's not – it's easier to do well than steak. Your aim is to lift the temperature of the pan slowly and not to super high, so you render the fat to perfection to create a deep gold, crispy skin.

Duck

1. Trim the duck breasts ensuring a good coverage of fat.
2. Marinate in a little of the oil and half the herbs.
3. When ready, pan sear in a medium heat non-stick pan skin-side down until you render and crisp the fat. Then add the other half of the herbs and 2 slightly crushed garlic cloves.
4. Once you have achieved the correct colour add the butter and baste.
5. Remove from the pan and finish in the oven at 180°C for 4 to 6 minutes depending on size.
6. When you're ready, assemble the ingredients onto each plate to serve. You might like to make proper gravy to go with it. See page 142.

Caramelised cauliflower

1. Break the cauliflower into florets, cut each floret in half and place flat side down in a non-stick pan.
2. Add the herbs, garlic and half the butter.
3. Cover with a circle of silicon paper to make a cartouche 'lid' and cook the cauliflower, adding the remainder of the butter if needed.

Beetroot

1. Cook the beetroot in salted boiling water with the herbs until tender – this takes between 45 minutes and an hour.
2. Once cool, cut and shape into neat circles then finish in a pan with a little butter.

Baby fondant potatoes

1. First, cut your potatoes into any shape you like. I like to use a small cutter but you could cut your potato into large cubes.
2. Add butter to a small pot and start to melt it.
3. Add your potato pieces and begin to caramelise them. Once you achieve a golden colour turn the potato over to caramelise the other side.
4. Now add stock to cover the potato and place pan into an oven at 160°C for 10 minutes or until the potato is cooked.

83. Seared monkfish wrapped in Parma ham, with green vegetables and sautéed new potatoes

Monkfish is a lovely, meaty fish. You will find it more forgiving than a thin filleted fish in that it doesn't break up when it's being cooked. This recipe requires you to trim the fish and separate the two fillets from the centre bone. If you'd prefer not to do this, ask your fishmonger to help.

400g monkfish

4 slices of Parma ham

500g new potatoes

40g butter

Cooking oil

Salt and cracked black pepper

For the green vegetables

1/2 bunch of asparagus

1/2 savoy cabbage

100g peas

1 head of broccoli

1. The first job is to get the potatoes on the go. New potatoes are traditionally cooked in boiling water, but I think if you cook from cold you get a much more even cook. One thing for sure is that you need a proper pinch of salt.

2. Once the potatoes are cooked, pour into a colander and let them steam out. Never cool in cold water even if you are getting ahead and cooking the day before. Steaming out gives the potatoes a chance to dry out and you get a much better potato.

3. Now onto the green vegetables, which you will need to blanch and refresh. Page 9 will explain it all.

4. The next job is to wrap the fish in the ham; this helps protect the fish and retain the moisture.

5. Then cut the fish into portion-size pieces.

6. Preheat a non-stick pan big enough to fit the amount of fish you are cooking. You are looking for the pan to have a 'medium heat'. You're not looking for the pan to be too hot.

7. Once the pan is ready, add a tablespoon of oil, just enough to lightly cover the base of the pan.

8. When the oil is hot add the monkfish on the cut edge and give each side of the fish a couple of minutes in the pan.

9. Add a knob of butter and baste the fish in the foaming butter. Remove from the heat and allow to sit in the pan for 2 to 3 minutes.

10. The fish should now feel firm to the touch.

11. While the fish is cooking, in another pan start to sauté your potatoes. To do this cut the potatoes in half and place into the pan with a little oil on the cut edge. Allow them to cook and gain loads of colour, turn them over and cook on the skin side.

12. Season with salt and cracked black pepper, remove the pan from the heat and add a small knob of butter. Baste the potatoes in the butter.

13. Remove the potatoes from the pan and keep warm, add the blanched green vegetables to the same pan adding a little more butter if necessary.

14. Double check the seasoning and serve.

84. Pan roast duck with sautéed potatoes, green vegetables and pancetta

4 duck breasts, skin on
100g pancetta, diced
400g new potatoes
50g butter
Cooking oil
Salt and cracked black
   pepper

For the green vegetables
1 pack of French beans
1 head of broccoli

Here's another delicious duck recipe. I know lots of people struggle with it, but please don't be put off cooking duck. It's a great meat to work with and easy to buy in supermarkets. If you follow some simple rules it's very straightforward to get right.

1. The first job is to get the potatoes on the go. New potatoes are traditionally cooked in boiling water, but I think if you cook from cold you get a much more even cook. One thing for sure is that you need a proper pinch of salt.

2. Once the potatoes are cooked, pour into a colander and let them steam out. Never cool in cold water even if you are getting ahead and cooking the day before. Steaming out gives the potatoes a chance to dry out and you get a much better potato. Cut them in half when cooled and put to one side.

3. Now onto the green vegetables, which you will need to blanch and refresh. Page 9 will explain it all.

4. Preheat your oven to 200°C.

5. The next task is to prepare the duck. Take each breast and lightly score with a knife.

6. In a cold pan add a little oil then place each breast skin-side down. Turn on the heat and slowly cook the duck. As the pan heats, the fat from the duck will start to gradually melt; at this stage it is vital to control the heat.

7. This stage will take about 10 minutes. You are looking for a nice golden-brown skin that has its fat rendered down.

8. When you are happy with the colour, turn the breast over and cook on the other side for a couple of minutes.

9. Remove from the pan and set the pan to one side – you want it for cooking your potatoes in – and place the duck onto a roasting tray, then pop into the oven for 6 minutes.

10. Meanwhile, start to sauté your potatoes using the pan the duck was cooked in. Make sure you use the wonderful duck fat left in the pan! Put the potato halves into the pan with a little oil on the cut edge. Allow them to cook and gain loads of colour, turn them over and cook on the skin side.

11. Season with salt and cracked black pepper, remove the pan from the heat and add a small knob of butter. Baste the potatoes in the butter.

12. Remove the potatoes from the pan and keep warm, add the diced pancetta and cook for a few minutes.

continues on the next page

84. Pan roast duck with sautéed potatoes, green vegetables and pancetta

13. Then add the blanched green vegetables to the same pan, adding a little more butter if necessary.

14. Remove your duck from the oven. The next stage is vital: you need to rest the duck for about five minutes. Resting the duck will ensure you have a wonderfully pink duck breast that's evenly cooked and won't lose all its juices when carved.

15. Serve the duck with the potatoes sautéed in duck fat and your pancetta and green vegetables.

Gigot of lamb with salt baked baby potatoes

85. Gigot of lamb marinated in mustard, honey, lemon, fennel seed and rosemary with salt baked baby potatoes

The marinade part of this recipe helps make it truly special. So, plan in advance – you need to marinate the lamb for at least 2 hours, but overnight is best. The little baby salt-baked potatoes are wonderful, too. For me, the best part of a regular baked potato is the crispy baked skin, so when you bake baby potatoes you get so much more skin and crispiness. Always cook more than you think you will need: once you start eating them you won't want to stop.

For the lamb

4 x 225g lamb leg steaks, bone in gigot

4 cloves of garlic

4 tbsp honey

2 tsp fennel seeds, toasted

1 tbsp Dijon mustard

2 rosemary sprigs, finely chopped

2 tbsp quality oil

1 lemon, juiced and zested

Sea salt and ground black pepper

For the potatoes

1kg baby new potatoes

200g table salt

1 sprig rosemary

1 sprig thyme

30ml quality oil

100ml crème fraîche

20g chives, chopped

Lamb

1. Crush the garlic cloves to a smooth paste with a little sea salt.
2. Mix together the garlic, honey, mustard, rosemary, oil, lemon juice, fennel seeds and some freshly ground pepper in a shallow dish.
3. Add the lamb leg steaks, coat well and leave to marinate.
4. When you're ready, preheat a non-stick pan or skillet. Lift the lamb steaks out of the marinade and shake off any excess.
5. Season with salt and pepper. Pan sear the lamb fillets for 5 minutes on each side, basting once or twice with the leftover marinade, until browned on the outside and slightly pink in the centre.

Potatoes

1. Preheat the oven to 180°C.
2. Chop the rosemary and thyme.
3. Coat the potatoes with the oil and chopped herbs.
4. Pour the salt onto a baking tray then place the potatoes on top.
5. Bake for 20 to 25 minutes until the potatoes are soft and have a crisp skin.
6. Mix the chopped chives and crème fraîche.
7. Cross the top of the potatoes, push up and top with your chivy crème fraîche.

86. Fillet of salmon with a warm potato salad, capers, poached egg and asparagus

4 x 180g fresh salmon fillets

200g new potatoes, Jersey Royals when in season

1/2 pack of chives, chopped

20g butter, optional

3 tbsp capers

4 eggs

50ml white wine vinegar

1/2 bunch of asparagus

Salt and pepper

For the hollandaise sauce
See recipe on page 143.

The capers, chives and salmon give this recipe a tremendous flavour that pairs beautifully with the asparagus and poached egg. It makes for a perfect lunch in the early summer when asparagus is in season.

1. Place potatoes into a pan, cover with water, add a pinch of salt and put onto boil. Once boiling turn down to a simmer. When they are cooked, you will need to drain and slice them.

2. Fill a small pan three quarters full of water, add the white wine vinegar then give the water a little taste to make sure it's nice and sour. It's vital that the water has some acid in it as it helps to set the egg white. Place the small pan on to boil, once boiling turn down to a rolling simmer.

3. Place each egg into a ramekin and gently lower into the vinegar water and poach for 2 to 3 minutes.

4. Once cooked place into ice cold water. This gets rid of the vinegar taste and stops the egg cooking any further. Once cold drain onto a tea towel or kitchen paper. You can reheat later in a pot of fresh salted simmering water.

5. Now blanch and refresh your asparagus – see page 9 for how to do this – and cut into slices.

6. Season the salmon and pan fry for 4 to 5 minutes or until cooked.

7. In a clean pan sauté the sliced potatoes until crisp and golden, add the capers, asparagus and chopped chives. Finish with a little butter.

8. Place the chives, capers and potatoes in the centre of a wide bowl then top with the salmon and then the poached egg.

9. You can serve with hollandaise sauce if you choose. See page 143.

87. Smoked trout with green salad, pea purée, almonds and dried cured ham

300g cold smoked trout or salmon

4 slices of dry cured ham, dried out in a low oven

100g French beans

100g snap peas

1 pack of mixed salad leaves

50g flaked almonds, toasted

1/4 pack of dill, chopped

For the pea purée

300g frozen peas

50g butter

For the salad dressing

1 lemon, zested and juiced

1/4 pack of chives, chopped

100ml quality oil

The pea purée in this recipe creates a great base to the dish which helps hold the whole thing together. And the method of building the final dish by adding a little bit of each ingredient in layers guarantees that every mouthful is alive with flavour and texture.

1. The first thing you need to do is to make the pea purée. Blanch the peas in a pan of boiling salted water; this should only take a few minutes. As soon as the water comes back to the boil remove the peas and blend in the food processor with the 50g of butter. Taste and season.

2. The next thing to do is blanch and refresh the French beans and snap peas. Blanching and refreshing is vital as it ensures the vibrant colour of the vegetables comes out and stays lovely and green. See page 9 for how to do this.

3. With the lemon, oil and chives make your lemon dressing. First, zest the lemon. Then put the lemon into the microwave for 10 seconds, as this helps extract all the juice. Add the zest to the juice and slowly add the oil. Taste and adjust the seasoning, then finish with the chopped chives.

4. You are now ready to assemble the dish.

5. Use a little of the dressing to dress the blanched beans, snap peas and salad leaves. Spread a spoonful of pea purée onto the bottom of the plate, then place some of the smoked trout onto the plate with the beans, salad leaves, dill, almonds and dried ham, then do the same again building up as you go.

88. Smoked haddock with creamy leeks, spinach, mashed potatoes and crispy poached egg

It should be so simple, but I've seen some weird and wonderful ways to poach an egg. In this recipe you start by poaching the eggs. This might seem back to front, but my method means you can even poach the eggs the day before (if you do, store them on a j-cloth covered with cling film). Use the freshest eggs possible as this really helps make a good poached egg. Don't add salt to the water as this affects the egg white and breaks it down, and there's no need for the water in the pan to boil.

4 fillets of naturally smoked haddock, pale

1 leek

1/2 bag of baby spinach

250ml milk

100ml double cream

25g butter

1/2 pack of chives, finely chopped

5 eggs

100g panko breadcrumbs

100ml vinegar

100g flour

Cooking oil

Salt and cracked black pepper

For the mashed potato
See recipe on page 147

1. Put a medium pan of water on the hob and add a generous amount of vinegar. Taste the water and if you don't make a funny face you need to add more vinegar; it should be acidic.
2. Carefully crack 4 of your eggs into 4 separate little cups or ramekins. Then take your cup with the egg inside and slowly submerge the cup into the water. Once the cup is full of the hot water carefully release the egg from the cup. This way the egg is not dropped in the water, which keeps the yolk surrounded in the white.
3. Add all 4 eggs the same way.
4. After a few minutes the eggs should be ready. Use a slotted spoon to remove them from the water one at a time, then submerge into ice-cold water to stop the cooking process and wash away the vinegar.
5. Next start on your perfect mashed potatoes. See recipe on page 147.
6. Now cut your leek. Halve it through the middle lengthwise, then chop down. Always wash leeks under plenty of cold running water to get rid of any grit.
7. Take your smoked haddock and place it in a pan with enough of your milk to cover the fish (about 200ml). Pop pan onto the heat and poach slowly.
8. In a separate pan add your leek and butter and cook on a medium heat until the leek has wilted. Now add your spinach and half of your chopped chives. Season with salt and cracked black pepper and finish with a little of the cooking liquor from the haddock along with the double cream.
9. To breadcrumb your poached eggs, take 3 bowls. In the first one add the flour and a little salt; in the second add a raw beaten egg and a splash of milk; in the last one the panko breadcrumbs.
10. Now roll each of the cold poached eggs in the seasoned flour, next into the egg and milk and lastly into the breadcrumbs.
11. In a pan add some oil until it's a third full and heat to about 180°C. Carefully place the eggs one at a time into the hot oil until crisp.
12. Remove the poached haddock from the pan and serve with your creamed leeks, crispy poached eggs and mashed potatoes.

89. Peppered fillet of beef with a blue cheese, pickled celery and walnut salad

Steak is such a classic dish – and it's one of those with a real mystique around it. Experts like to debate the correct pans, cuts, cooking times . . . I hope this recipe proves straightforward, enjoyable and tasty. It's up to you how you like your steak cooked, and this is determined by how long you seal the meat and leave it in the pan. With a fillet I suggest popping it in the oven for a few minutes unless you like your steak blue or rare.

4 x 160g beef fillet steaks

50ml cooking oil

1 tsp cracked black pepper

A few flakes of sea salt

A drizzle of quality oil

For the pickled celery

2 sticks of celery, peeled and cut into fine strips

70ml white wine vinegar

50g honey

2 sprigs of thyme

For the salad

1 carrot, peeled and cut into fine strips

100g blue cheese, crumbled

2 slices of bread

20g butter

A handful of mixed salad leaves

75g walnuts

1. Your first job is to take the steak out of the fridge and bring it to room temperature.
2. Next, sort the salad. Start with the pickled celery. Put your vinegar and honey into a pot with the thyme, bring to the boil, and then check the balance: it should have a pleasant sweet pickle flavour.
3. Remove from the heat and add your celery strips to the pickling liquid.
4. Next cut your bread into a fine dice and pan fry in a little butter until crisp. Now you have some homemade croutons!
5. In a bowl add your mixed leaves, cut carrot, crispy croutons, pickled celery, cheese and your walnuts, put to one side.
6. Now it's time to cook your steak.
7. First preheat the oven to 200°C, and then heat a heavy-based non-stick pan or griddle on a high heat, adding a touch of oil.
8. Once the pan is hot, the oil will start to haze slightly. Season the steak with flaked sea salt and cracked black pepper.
9. Add the steak to the pan. You are 'sealing' the meat, which is all about creating colour and flavour. Resist the urge to shake the pan as this will cool the pan down and you'll end up boiling the meat.
10. Remember, if the pan cools down the juices come out. And if the juices come out you lose colour and moisture. Allow your steak a few minutes on each side depending how well you like it cooked.
11. Next allow the steak to rest. This allows the meat to settle and lets the juices relax giving you a much more flavoursome meat with a beautiful blush and even colour.
12. Drizzle a little quality oil over the top of your bowl of salad and toss until everything is mixed.
13. Serve your fillet with your beautiful salad.

90. Fillet of red mullet with fondant potatoes and warm gazpacho

This is a wonderful dish, very fresh and light. Gazpacho is famous as a cold Spanish soup; here I use its essence to create a sauce that works very well with red mullet. The sauce can be warmed or served at room temperature – it's up to you. The fish is pan fried – and the secret here is not to prod at the fish when it's in the pan. People often prod the fish, realise it is stuck and panic. In truth, almost every time you pan fry fish it sticks. But, if you have a little patience and leave it alone, the fish skin will crisp up and unstick itself from the pan.

8 fillets of red mullet,
  scaled and pin boned

4 ripe plum tomatoes

25g tomato purée

1/4 cucumber, finely diced

1/2 red pepper, finely
  diced

1 red chilli, finely diced

1 red onion, finely diced

1/2 bunch of basil

1 bag of baby spinach

25g butter

Quality oil

Sugar, to taste

Salt and cracked
  black pepper

Lemon, juiced, to serve

For the fondant potatoes
See recipe on page 148

1. In a blender blitz the plum tomatoes and the tomato purée.
2. Then pass this liquid through a sieve and double check the balance of flavour. It might need a little sugar, salt and pepper to bring out the full tomato flavour.
3. Next shred the basil and add to the tomato mix.
4. Add the diced cucumber, red chilli, red pepper and red onion to the tomato mix. You should now have a bright and fresh-looking sauce.
5. Take a little butter and place it into a pan. Once melted, add the spinach and wilt down, then season with some freshly cracked black pepper.
6. Now cook the fish. Pop a pan on the stove, add a little oil and wait until the pan starts to have a slight haze. Place the mullet fillets skin-side down to pan fry.
7. Cook the fish for 90% of the time in the pan until the skin is crispy, then carefully turn it over and remove the pan from the heat. Squeeze in some lemon juice and add a little knob of butter. Baste the fish in the lemony butter, then serve with your fondant potatoes, buttered spinach and gazpacho sauce.

91. Confit duck legs with green lentils

For the confit duck

4 duck legs and thigh
joints

400g duck fat, or enough
to totally submerge the
duck legs

6 cumin seeds

12 coriander seeds

3 juniper berries

50g flaky sea salt

1 bunch of thyme

1 sprig of rosemary

1 clove of garlic, sliced

2 bay leaves

1 tsp black peppercorns

For the lentils

300g green lentils

100g pancetta

50g butter

2 tbsp quality oil

1 onion, finely chopped

1 garlic clove, finely sliced

1 carrot, diced

1 stick of celery, diced

1 courgette, diced

175ml red wine

450ml beef stock

2 tbsp sherry vinegar

2 tbsp flat parsley,
chopped

Many consider duck confit to be one of the finest French dishes. It's a superb way to impress at a dinner party. You need to plan in advance; it's essential you leave the duck to marinate in its spice and herb mix for at least 24 hours.

Confit duck

1. The day before cooking, put the cumin and coriander seeds in a dry pan and toast until they are slightly coloured and aromatic.
2. Remove to a board and crush them with the blade of a knife.
3. Crush the juniper berries and mix with the spices and the salt.
4. Rub the mixture over the duck, scatter with thyme, rosemary and sliced garlic and chill for 24 hours. Remember to turn two or three times as they marinate.
5. The next day, heat the oven to 150°C.
6. Wipe the duck with kitchen paper and pat dry, but don't wash off the marinade.
7. Put the duck in a cast-iron casserole dish and cover with the duck fat.
8. Add the bay leaves and peppercorns and cook for about 2.5 hours, or until the meat is almost falling away from the bone.
9. At this stage, you can store the duck simply by placing it in a pudding bowl, covering it with the fat and keeping it in the fridge: as long as it stays covered with fat it will last for weeks.
10. To cook, remove the confit duck legs from their fat. Put an ovenproof frying pan on the stove until it is hot. Add the duck legs, skin-side down, and cook for 4 minutes. Turn the legs and transfer the pan to the oven for 30 minutes, until crisp.

Lentils

1. Heat a sauté pan or a large frying pan, then add the butter and oil. Once hot, add the onion and cook for 2 minutes.
2. Add the pancetta, garlic, carrot and celery and cook for 4 minutes more.
3. Add the lentils and red wine and bring to the boil. Cook until the wine has reduced by half then add the stock and cook the lentils for 25 to 30 minutes. Mix in the sherry vinegar, chopped parsley and diced courgette.
4. To finish place the confit duck on its bed of lentils. *Bon appetit!*

92. **Venison Wellington** with new potatoes and buttered baby carrots

500g venison loin

1 sheet of butter puff pastry

1 pack of chestnut mushrooms, chopped

Butter, for cooking

1 banana shallot, chopped

2 cloves of garlic, chopped

3 sprigs of thyme, picked

1/4 savoy cabbage

12 baby carrots

500g new potatoes

3 eggs

100g plain flour

50ml milk

Quality oil

Salt and pepper, to season

This recipe has lots of elements, but don't worry – all of them are quite straightforward. Even the crêpes. Although for some reason the first crêpe you make is never as good as the second.

1. Firstly, season the loin of venison.
2. Now, heat some oil in a frying pan and sear the meat all over until you have achieved good colour on every surface of the meat.
3. Next, start on your mushroom mix, which is known as a duxelle. Melt the butter and soften the shallot and garlic. Add the chopped mushrooms, herbs and seasoning, and cook until you have a paste-like mixture. The time this takes depends on the moisture of the mushrooms. Leave to cool.
4. Next blanch and refresh your cabbage leaves. Page 9 tells you how.
5. Now make 2 French crêpes. Take 2 eggs, a splash of milk and a drop of oil; then whisk in enough flour until you get a thin batter consistency.
6. Take a hot frying pan with a little oil. Now pour the batter mix into the pan and swirl until the mix creates a thin layer.
7. Cook the crêpe in the pan and turn over. You'll need to do this twice.
8. Overlap 2 or 3 sheets of cling film on a clean surface and lay the two crêpes, slightly overlapping, on each one.
9. Take some of your blanched cabbage leaves and dry them off with kitchen paper. Lay the cabbage onto the crêpes.
10. Spread the cooled mushroom mix all over the cabbage leaves, creating a thin, even layer.
11. Place the venison in the centre of the mushroom mix. Using the edge of the cling film, carefully wrap the crêpe, cabbage and mushroom mix around the fillet. Roll into a sausage shape.
12. Twist the ends of the cling film one side clockwise then the other anticlockwise to form a tight log. Chill in the fridge for 30 minutes.
13. Meanwhile cook your potatoes and baby carrots. See page 169 for how to do this.
14. On a lightly floured surface, place the pre-rolled puff pastry.
15. Unwrap your venison log from the fridge and lie it in the middle of the pastry. Fold over the bottom half of the pastry. Lightly brush the rest of the sheet with beaten egg. Roll the whole thing around the meat to encase. Neatly trim the edges to create a parcel
16. Transfer to a baking sheet and brush all over with beaten egg yolk.
17. Leave to chill for at least 30 minutes and, at the same time, preheat your oven to 200°C.
18. Use the back of a knife to mark the pastry, being careful not to cut all the way through.
19. Bake for 25 to 30 minutes, then remove from the oven and rest for 20 minutes. Serve with your potatoes and vegetables.

93. **Baked Camembert** with a granary, rosemary and hazelnut crumb and red onion chutney

For the chutney

3 medium red onions

1 red chilli, finely chopped

50g sultanas

2 cloves of garlic, finely chopped

50g light brown sugar

1 tbsp quality oil

100ml red wine vinegar

50ml port

2 bay leaves

1 tsp coriander seeds

1/2 stick of cinnamon, broken up

Square of muslin and string to make spice bag

For the Camembert

1 Camembert cheese, in wooden box

75g hazelnuts

2 sprigs of rosemary, picked and chopped

8 slices of granary bread

1 shallot, finely diced

20g butter

This is the ultimate baked Camembert – always a sure-fire winner with guests on any occasion. No one can resist this combination of gorgeously gooey cheese with its nutty crumb, toasty soldiers and sticky chutney.

Red onion chutney

1. Your first job is to peel and halve the onions through the root. Then slice the onion by cutting with the grain. Try to avoid the rainbow cut as the onion breaks down too much if you do this.

2. Heat the oil in a large pan on a low heat. Now add the onions, chilli, garlic, sultanas and bay leaves and cook gently for 20 minutes stirring occasionally.

3. Make a spice bag using a small square of muslin and a piece of string. Simply wrap up all spices, tie tight and add to the pan.

4. Once the onions are cooked and translucent, add the sugar, vinegar and port and stir well. Then simmer on a low heat for 30 to 40 minutes, stirring occasionally until the chutney is wonderfully thick, dark and sticky.

5. Remove the spice bag.

6. You can use the chutney straight away, or store in a sterilised jar; an old jam jar is perfect for this.

Baked Camembert

1. Preheat your oven to 180°C.

2. Remove your Camembert from its packaging, then place it back into the wooden box after removing the plastic wrapper.

3. Take two slices of the bread and place into a food processor to blitz into breadcrumbs.

4. Place your hazelnuts on a tray and put them into the oven at 160°C for 6 to 8 minutes. When you take them from the oven pour them onto a clean tea towel, close up the fabric to make a little bag and rub the hazelnuts together. This will remove the skins from the nuts.

5. Add the nuts to the bread in the processor and break them down.

6. Along with a little of the butter sweat down the chopped shallot in a pan, then add some chopped rosemary, breadcrumbs and nuts.

7. Carefully cook this mixture in the pan until you start to achieve a little colour. Remove from the heat.

continues on the next page

93. Baked Camembert with a granary, rosemary and hazelnut crumb and red onion chutney

8. Make bread 'soldiers' by cutting the remaining 6 slices of bread into the required shape.

9. In a frying pan add the rest of your butter and a little chopped rosemary. Heat the pan slowly until the butter starts to crackle, then add the cut bread and cook until the bread starts to crisp up. You need to control the heat of the pan very carefully so you don't burn the butter.

10. Top the Camembert with some of the hazelnut crumb and then place into the oven. At first you won't actually notice anything happen. What you want to achieve is a slow process of melting the cheese from within.

11. Every now and then give the cheese a little wobble and you will start to see that the cheese is melting. After about 15 to 20 minutes in the oven it will be perfect.

12. Serve with your toasted soldiers and red onion chutney

94. Slow cooked belly of pork with balsamic onions and caponata

For the pork

1kg pork belly, rind removed

1 onion, roughly chopped

1 carrot, peeled and chopped

1/2 packet of thyme

30ml quality oil

1 tsp paprika

1/2 tsp chilli powder

1/2 tsp ground cumin

150ml vegetable stock

For the caponata

1 aubergine, cut into 1 cm dice

1 onion, chopped

2 sticks of celery, peeled and cut into 1 cm dice

1 courgette, cut into 1 cm dice

2 plum tomatoes, chopped

50g sultanas

50g pine nuts

100ml quality oil

50ml red wine vinegar

1 tbsp sugar

1/2 bunch of basil, to finish

Salt and pepper

For the balsamic onions

200g baby onions, peeled

75ml balsamic vinegar

50g honey

4 sprigs of thyme

Here is a fabulous belly of pork recipe for you to try. This time with caponata which is a beautifully flavoursome Sicilian dish that complements the warm spices of the pork belly. It's a good idea to create the balsamic onions and the caponata while the pork belly is cooking.

Pork

1. Preheat your oven to 130°C.
2. Take the pork belly and rub in the oil, then gradually rub in the spices and a little salt.
3. Place your chopped vegetables and thyme into a deep roasting tray, pop the pork onto the top then pour in the vegetable stock, cover the tray with a couple of sheets of tinfoil and bake in the oven for 2 to 2.5 hours.
4. Once cooked carefully remove the pork from the tray and place into another tray. Then put a clean tray on top of the hot pork and, with a couple of cans, press the belly until cold.
5. Once cold the pork can be cut and reheated when needed.

Caponata

1. Put the oil into a large pan, then once it's hot add the onion, aubergine, celery and courgette.
2. Cook down at a high heat until you have achieved some colour.
3. Add the sultanas, pine nuts and lower the heat and cook for 10 minutes.
4. Next add the chopped tomatoes, red wine vinegar and sugar.
5. Cook the stew for another 10 minutes, double check the seasoning, garnish with basil leaves and put to one side.

Balsamic onions

1. Pop the onions into a small pan with the honey, thyme and vinegar.
2. Slowly cook the onions until tender.
3. Have a taste to check the sweet and sourness, and adjust with more vinegar or honey as feels right.

KIDS' KITCHEN

First things first. Feeding kids is not easy. I sometimes find it difficult to please my kids at dinnertime. I believe kids are smart, curious creatures who want to find out the finest details about everything. I also find that the older your kids get the more their tastes and opinions change, but the rules are still the same.

You won't find this chapter filled with ways to hide 'healthy' food within 'fun' food or ways to make happy faces or Jenga towers out of carrots and broccoli. What you will find is food that I think kids will love to help you with. Loads of hands-on shaping and rolling jobs that can keep them busy while you get the bulk of the work done. And, for me, one fundamental thing is: kids should be eating the same food as you, alongside you.

The key to expanding your kids' dish count is to get them involved as much as possible in all things related to food. It can start in the shops: let your kids pick their food, let them have a wee wander around the vegetable section. Better still, if you have a couple of kids let them each pick different vegetables and you will find they soon become very competitive with each other about whose is the best! Ultimately the result is a win for everyone – your kids will be happy to eat the vegetables once they have an investment in and connection with them. So, if it starts in the shop, I then let the kids follow the journey of the food to the plate. Helping put the food away, storing the food, getting them involved in preparation every now and again even if they are not totally hands on. Just let them know what you are doing with their food, let them have a peek into the pot or the oven, stir a cake in the bowl, or grind spices in the pestle and mortar. If you treat kids like little adults and don't make food a mystery then of course it helps them understand it better. I really believe that hiding food from our kids is half the problem.

I know it's unrealistic to expect that every time you go shopping and cook dinner you'll have your kids fully involved, but once a child has learned about a specific food or ingredient they'll then trust and understand that ingredient, and everyone's happy because they are more likely to embrace the dish.

Of course, the truth is that these thoughts about engaging kids with food is how we've been behaving and interacting for thousands of years – we've always been passing life skills on to the next generation. It seems to me that it's only in recent history that learning to cook from a parent, grandparent, aunty or neighbour has stopped being an essential part of growing up. In the UK at least, our whole family and community structure has changed dramatically since the Second World War, and the shared heritage of passing on the skill of cooking has diminished for many.

I really believe teaching our kids to cook is one of the most important jobs of a parent – or any adult entrusted with the care of young children. Cooking is a life skill that actually means life.

95. Miso cured salmon rolls with toasted sesame seeds

A quarter side of salmon

Miso paste, to marinate

10g sesame seeds, toasted

10g black sesame seeds

1 sheet of leaf gelatine

1/2 tsp curry powder

1/2 tsp cumin

1/4 pack of watercress, or other salad leaf to top

10g wasabi, as a dip

Salt and pepper

A steamer, plus a temperature probe if you have one

This is a fantastic dish for kids to get 'hands on' with fish. Salmon is fairly robust and can cope with being manhandled by little hands. Even if the kids are too young to do the actual rolling, they can be totally involved in sprinkling the herbs and adding seasoning. Once cooked and cut, these rolls are brilliant for kids to enjoy little bite-sized morsels.

1. Cut the salmon into long strips and marinate in some miso.
2. Season with the curry powder, cumin, salt and pepper.
3. Lay a large piece of cling film onto your work surface.
4. Place one length of the salmon onto the cling film.
5. Cut the sheet of gelatine in half length-wise and place on top of the salmon. Then place another strip of salmon on top of that. The gelatine between the salmon will glue both pieces together once cooked.
6. Roll the lengths of salmon in the spice mix tightly and tie both ends of the film.
7. When ready place in the steamer. The temperature you use depends on how you like your salmon cooked. I cook it to 53°C, which achieves a perfectly moist, tasty salmon.
8. Once the salmon is cooked how you like it, allow it to cool and then set in the fridge.
9. Once set, remove from the film and wrap in sesame seeds, then rewrap in film as this will help with the cutting.
10. Cut to size when needed, top your salad leaves and enjoy.

96. Spinach and ricotta tortellini with ham hock, tomato and chilli

This is a great recipe to plan in advance. I suggest you soak the ham hock in cold water for a few hours to rid it of any excess salt. You can also cook it the day before, especially if you're not using a pressure cooker; the ham will happily keep once cooked. Making tortellini with kids is brilliant – you can get a proper production line going and to see the pile of homemade shapes at the end is really satisfying.

For the fresh pasta
See recipe on page 61

For the pesto
See recipe on page 138

Other ingredients

1 smoked ham hock, pancetta also works

1 packet of cherry tomatoes, cut in half

2 red chillies, sliced

50g ricotta cheese

50ml quality oil

1 egg, beaten

For the filling

1 bag of baby spinach, stalks removed

20g butter

200g ricotta cheese

50g Parmesan cheese, grated

A pinch of paprika

1. First, soak the ham hock in cold water for a couple of hours.
2. When it's ready, cook in a pressure cooker for about 40 minutes. If you don't have one, simmer it gently for about two hours – until the meat's falling off the bone.
3. Next you need to sort the filling for the tortellini. In a pan wilt most of the spinach with a little butter, then remove from the heat. Once cool, squeeze out any water, add 200g of your ricotta, a pinch of paprika and all of your grated Parmesan cheese.
4. Mix and double check the seasoning. Put in the fridge until needed.
5. Now put the cherry tomato halves and sliced red chillies to one side.
6. Now onto your tortellini. Roll your pasta out as thin as you can, then use an 8 cm cutter to cut as many circles of pasta as you can. You'll need to get the cuts as close to each other as possible.
7. Stack the circles on top of each other to stop them from drying out.
8. Make the tortellini one at a time until you get the hang of it. Take a pasta circle, put in about half a teaspoon of your ricotta and spinach filling, then use a pastry brush and the beaten egg to brush around half the pasta circle.
9. Lift the circle of pasta off the surface and carefully fold in half. Make sure you get out as much air as possible before you join the ends.
10. Place what is now a semicircle of pasta onto your surface and use the back of a 5 cm cutter to press the pasta to create a seal between the filling and the edge of the semicircle.
11. Pick the pasta back up and carefully wrap the ends of the pasta around your finger to create a hole and the iconic tortellini shape.
12. Repeat this until you have used all the filling. Once you get into the swing of it you can probably do about five at a time.
13. When all your tortellini is ready, cook in salted boiling water for about three minutes and then refresh in cold running water.
14. In a large pan add a little oil with the remainder of the spinach, the tomatoes and red chilli.
15. Once it has all started to wilt add the cooked ham and pasta and mix carefully.
16. Serve with a little pesto and the remainder of the ricotta cheese.

97. Pizza with chestnut mushrooms, red onion, chilli and mozzarella

For the dough

450g pizza flour
  or bread flour

300g water at 37˚C, baby
  bottle temperature

10g quality oil

5g sea salt

1 sachet of dried yeast

Parchment paper

For the sauce

400g tin of tomatoes

100g tomato purée

2 cloves of garlic

50ml quality oil

1 tsp mixed herbs, dried

2 tbsp of sugar

Salt and pepper, to taste

For the topping

1 pack of baby mozzarella

1 pack of chestnut
  mushrooms, sliced

1 red onion, cut into
  wedges

2 red chillies, deseeded
  and chopped

Cooking oil

Leaves from a small bunch
  of basil, to finish

It's great to make pizzas from scratch – especially because making dough is one of those cooking activities kids love. You'll see I don't cook my pizza sauce. The freshness of the tomato is better retained if it's only cooked once: on top of the pizza. On the other hand, I find it vital to part-cook any vegetables that go on top of a pizza. The pizza itself takes a matter of minutes to cook, which isn't long enough for the vegetables to cook properly.

Pizza dough

1. Sieve the flour and salt into a bowl.
2. Mix the water, yeast and oil together.
3. Make a well in the centre of the flour and add the water, yeast and oil mixture.
4. Mix the ingredients together with a spoon until it forms a loose dough.
5. Knead the dough until smooth and firm to the touch. It won't take long and you'll know it's good to go when you press it with your thumb and it bounces back.
6. Put the dough back into the bowl, cover with cling film and let it double in size. This should take about 20 minutes. There's no need to put the dough into a warm place; your house is warm enough.
7. You are now ready to ball the dough.
8. Remove 240g of dough per ball, but don't use a knife. I think of the process as like strangling a ball from the dough with your hands.
9. Ball all your dough, then place onto a tray and cover with cling film.
10. Next, roll the pizzas out. You can do this a number of ways. A pizza chef will do what's called 'pushing the dough', which involves shaping the dough without using a rolling pin. I am rubbish at that, so I use a rolling pin.
11. Once it's the correct thickness, place the rolled dough onto parchment paper. This is so you can move the dough once it's got all its toppings on. You might wonder, why not just build your pizza on a tray and put that in the oven? It's because you want the base to hit a very hot tray to create a crispy base.

Pizza sauce

1. Combine all ingredients and purée with a hand blender.
2. Check the seasoning. It should taste lovely and fresh with a good balance between sweet and bitter.

Pizza toppings

1. Put your red onion and chillies in a non-stick pan with a little oil. Cook at a high heat until you have achieved some colour.
2. Remove from the pan and add your sliced mushrooms to the pan for a few minutes; again you are looking to achieve colour.

To create your pizzas

1. Spoon sauce onto your rolled pizza base. Don't put too much sauce on as you'll end up with a soggy pizza. A little goes a long way.
2. Start to build your toppings. I like the little mozzarella balls as they are easy to portion and divide between your pizzas.
3. Once you have topped your pizza carefully lift it with the parchment paper and place onto a hot tray.
4. Bake at 220°C to 250°C until your pizza is crisp and golden.

98. Pizza with mozzarella pearls, red chilli and basil pesto

These delicious little pizzas make a brilliant alternative for anyone who doesn't enjoy the tomatoes in a regular pizza. Kids like blending all the ingredients to make the pesto, which you can keep for pasta for tea the next day!

For the pesto
70g basil
50g Parmesan, grated
50g pine nuts, toasted
2 cloves of garlic
2 tbsp quality oil
Salt, to taste

For the topping
1 pack of baby mozzarella
2 red chillies, deseeded and chopped

Pesto

1. Blend the basil with half the oil and a pinch of salt.
2. Add the toasted pine nuts then blend in the garlic.
3. Finally add the Parmesan and blend with the rest of the oil.

Pizza dough

1. Use the ingredients and follow the steps in recipe 97 on page 198 for your pizza dough.

To create your pizzas

1. Spoon pesto onto your rolled pizza base. Don't put too much as you'll end up with a soggy pizza. Again, a little goes a long way.
2. Start to build your cheese and chilli topping. I like the little mozzarella balls as they are easy to portion and divide between your pizzas.
3. Once you have topped your pizza carefully lift the pizza with the parchment paper and place onto a hot tray.
4. Bake at 220°C to 250°C until your pizza is crisp and golden.

99. Crispy Mull haggis with red onion chutney, mashed tatties and roasted turnip

For the Mull haggis
300g haggis, from the supermarket or butcher

4 sheets of filo pastry

1 egg, for the egg wash

For the roasted turnip
1 turnip

20g butter

For the red onion chutney
20ml cooking oil

3 red onions, sliced

3 sprigs of thyme, picked and chopped

50ml port or red wine

1 tbsp redcurrant jelly

For the mashed tatties
2 large potatoes

25g double cream

15g butter

Pinch of nutmeg

Seasoning, to taste

Haggis, neeps and tatties is a Burns Night classic. I created this recipe for *MasterChef*, where it was declared the smartest version of this traditional dish that you'll ever taste! Why not make an occasion of it with your family?

Mull haggis
1. Break down the haggis in a food processor, then roll into strips that are approximately 15 cm long and 10 mm thick.
2. Halve the sheets of filo pastry, wash with the egg, then lay on the haggis and roll up tightly.
3. When you are ready to serve, shallow fry your pastry and haggis roll until crisp.

Roasted turnip
1. Peel and cut the turnip into medium dice.
2. Place into a pan with the butter and slowly cook, basting the turnip with butter as you go.
3. Once cooked, put to one side.

Red onion chutney
1. Add the sliced red onion to a thick-bottomed pan with the oil and cook down gently for 10 minutes.
2. Add the port, redcurrant jelly and chopped thyme.
3. Cook until beautifully reduced and sticky.

Mashed tatties
1. Cut and cook your potatoes as for the Perfect Mash recipe on page 147, but instead of adding egg, etc. you need to . . .
2. Beat in the cream and butter, add a pinch of nutmeg and adjust the seasoning.

100. Thai crab cakes with avocado and spiced mayonnaise

For the crab cakes

100g white crab meat

100g white fish

1 bunch of coriander, finely shredded

2 red chillies, finely diced

1 lime, zested and juiced

1 lemon grass stalk

50g root ginger

1 egg white

Soy sauce, Habhal is perfect

Fish sauce, just a dash

Cooking oil

For the avocado

1 avocado, ripe

1 red chilli, finely diced

8 leaves of basil, shredded

1 lime, juiced

For the spiced mayonnaise

200ml mayonnaise

1 red chilli, finely diced

50ml chilli sauce

50ml tomato ketchup

Tabasco sauce, 5 or 6 drops

Kids can't get enough of eating these bite-size crab cakes with their hands! They have all the delicious, light and spicy flavours you would expect from Thailand. To get them just right, take the time before you start shaping all the mix to cook a little off so you can check and adjust the seasoning. You can use any white fish – for example, haddock, cod or hake – whatever your fishmonger recommends.

Crab cakes

1. Double check your white crab meat to ensure you don't have any shell.
2. To prepare your lemon grass for this dish you are looking to get the heart of the lemon grass. This is the first couple of layers from the inside where they are nice and soft. Chop as finely as possible.
3. To prepare your ginger, peel it with the edge of a spoon as this reduces waste and is easier than using a knife. You now have two options: either grate it through a fine grater, or slice very thinly, cut into matchsticks then cut the matchsticks into fine dice.
4. Blitz the white fish in a food processor, then add the egg white, lime juice and zest, lemon grass, ginger and coriander.
5. Remove and place into a bowl. Add a few drops of soy sauce and fish sauce, and the crab meat, then mix.
6. Once you're happy with the seasoning, shape the mix into small 6 cm patties and pan fry in a hot frying pan until golden in colour.
7. Serve with the avocado and spiced mayonnaise.

Avocado

1. Remove the flesh from the avocado by placing it on a cutting board and inserting a knife into the skin from the top until you hit the stone. Then work your way around the stone until you have cut all the way around.
2. Twist the avocado and the two halves should separate. One half will have the stone in, so with the back of a cook's knife carefully tap the stone and twist. It can now be removed.
3. Remove the flesh from the avocado with a spoon and crush with a fork. Then add the basil, chilli and lime.

Spiced mayonnaise

1. Mix all ingredients together and adjust seasoning.

101. Manchego-stuffed bread parcels

For the dough

450g strong bread flour

1 sachet of fast acting yeast

1 tbsp sugar

1 tsp table salt

300g water at 37°C, baby bottle temperature

To flavour

1 red onion, sliced

200g Manchego cheese, grated

1 small bunch of thyme

Quality oil

Sea salt, to sprinkle

Nigella seeds, to sprinkle

Kids love to knead and I'm sure that's partly because there's no right or wrong way to do it. As long as you're working the dough around the surface, stretching and pulling for 5 to 10 minutes, you're doing a good job. The more you work the dough the firmer and smoother it becomes, which is an indication that it's ready.

1. Place the flour and salt into a bowl and mix well. Then make a well in the centre.
2. Add the yeast and sugar to the water and mix until dissolved.
3. Slowly incorporate the flour and yeast solution together until you have a rough dough.
4. Don't put your hands into the mixture as you'll end up with half a kilo of dough on your fingers! Use a spoon or spatula to bring the mixture together.
5. At this stage the flour has absorbed the water, but we haven't yet developed the gluten protein to make it a smooth firm dough.
6. Lightly flour a work surface and tip the dough out and begin to knead.
7. A good way to test the dough is to take your index finger and gently press it. If it springs back it's ready; if the indentation stays then work the dough longer.
8. When ready place back in the bowl, cover with cling film and allow to rest at room temperature until doubled in size. This normally takes 35 to 45 minutes depending on the temperature of your kitchen.
9. Meanwhile, caramelise the onion. Slice evenly, put in a frying pan with a little oil and gently cook on a low heat until sticky and caramelised. Allow to cool.
10. Next, tip the dough out of its bowl and knock it back just for a minute or two.
11. To shape the bread cut the dough into 40g pieces and then roll out into thin oval shapes. Place the ovals onto on a flat non-stick baking tray, then line the centre of the dough with the cooled caramelised onion and a scattering of Manchego cheese.
12. Fold in the top corner to meet the centre and fold the opposite corner on top. Repeat this process for the other corners and you should be left with a diamond in the middle of the bread where the onion and cheese are exposed.
13. Drizzle with oil, a good pinch of sea salt, a sprinkle of fresh thyme and Nigella seeds.
14. Cover with cling film again and prove the bread for 15 to 20 minutes or until the bread has again nearly doubled in size. Proving will be quicker this time as the yeast has been activated in the resting stage.
15. Bake in a preheated oven at 190°C for 18 minutes.

102. Potato and Parmesan gnocchi
with wild mushrooms, grilled courgettes, pear and herb dressing

400g Maris Piper
  potatoes

120g bread flour

50g Parmesan, grated

1 egg yolk

100g mixed wild
  mushrooms

1/2 courgette, sliced

1 Williams pear, cut into
  matchsticks

1/4 pack of chives,
  chopped

1 lemon, juiced

100ml quality oil

Salt and pepper, to season

This recipe uses homemade gnocchi – and I promise if you haven't tried it before then you're in for a real treat. My children love the 'production line' element to making lots of little gnocchi shapes: it's a really satisfying way to work together in the kitchen.

1. First, make the gnocchi. You will need to cook and mash the potatoes using the Perfect Mash recipe on page 147 until you get to . . .

2. Put your mashed potato into a large bowl, add the egg yolk and grated Parmesan.

3. Then start to work in the flour. With your hands, incorporate enough flour until you get a workable consistency. You might need more or less of the flour depending on how much moisture the potatoes have.

4. Next take some of your mix and with a little flour roll out a long sausage shape. Cut this into even-sized pieces and add a little indentation with a fork. These are your gnocchi!

5. Cook them in boiling salted water until they float. This takes about a minute, but you might have to do this in stages so you don't overcrowd the pot.

6. Once ready, remove the gnocchi with a slotted spoon and refresh in cold water.

7. Now make your dressing. Mix 75ml of oil with the juice of half a lemon, chopped chives, then season and put to one side.

8. Next, in a large frying pan with a little oil, fry your gnocchi until you create a golden crust. Remove them from the pan and add your mushrooms, adding a little more oil if need be.

9. Meanwhile griddle your courgette slices. If you don't have a griddle pan fry them with the mushrooms.

10. Put your gnocchi back into the pan and add a few teaspoons of the dressing and a squeeze of lemon, to taste.

11. Top with some pear matchsticks to serve.

103. Smoked haddock, chive and mustard croquettes with leek and potato broth

For the croquettes

500g potatoes, peeled and cut into quarters

25g butter

50g wholegrain mustard

300g smoked haddock, pale smoked is best

1/4 pack of chives, chopped

100g plain flour, seasoned

2 eggs, beaten with some milk

100g panko breadcrumbs

500ml milk

For the broth

100g white of leek, sliced and diced

1/2 onion, finely chopped

400g potatoes, peeled and diced into 1/2 cm chunks

50g butter

50g double cream

1/4 pack of chives, chopped

50g wholegrain mustard

Smoked haddock milk, as saved

White truffle oil, optional

This is another recipe where kids enjoy getting hands on with all the elements of the 'production line'! You can cook these croquettes in a few different ways, but if you deep-fry them they will have a crispy outer shell which is a lovely contrast to the creamy broth.

Smoked haddock croquettes

1. In a large pan cook your potatoes in cold salted water that you slowly bring to the boil. Try not to overcook as they will end up water logged, making the croquettes hard to work with.
2. Once cooked, drain the potatoes and allow to 'steam out' for a few minutes. Then place them back into the pot and put it back onto the stove on a low heat to dry them out.
3. Now add the butter and the wholegrain mustard, then mash. You can use a traditional potato masher, but you will get a much better result with a potato ricer.
4. Take the haddock and have a feel for bones. You sometimes find them running down the middle or at the sides at the top.
5. Place the haddock into a pan with the milk and slowly bring to the boil. Once the milk has come to the boil turn off the heat. Save the cooking liquor.
6. Before everything gets cold mix the fish into the potato mash, add the chives and check for seasoning.
7. Shape the mixture into a long sausage shape and cut to croquette size. You are now ready to coat in breadcrumbs.
8. You need three bowls: one with seasoned flour, another with the eggs and the milk, and lastly one for the breadcrumbs.
9. Start with the flour, roll the croquettes in it, then roll them in the egg and milk mixture and then the breadcrumbs. The theory is the flour will stick to the croquette, the egg and milk stick to the flour and the breadcrumbs to the egg and milk.
10. You are now ready to cook. You could deep fry until golden, or shallow fry making sure you keep them moving, or you could spray them with a little oil and bake them in a hot oven at 180°C.

Leek and potato broth

1. Melt the butter in a deep pan, add the leek and onion and cook without colour for a few minutes, stirring occasionally with a wooden spatula.
2. Add the potatoes and the smoked haddock milk.
3. Bring to the boil and simmer until all the ingredients are tender. Try not to cook for too long as you want the potatoes to keep their shape.
4. Bring back to a simmer and finish with the double cream, mustard and a drizzle of white truffle oil and chopped chives and split between your dishes. To serve, top with the haddock croquettes.

104. Sushi rolls

400g sushi rice

450ml water

6 tbsp rice wine vinegar

2 tbsp sugar

2 tsp salt

1 pack of nori seaweed
sheets

Pickled ginger

For the fillings

Spring onions

Enoki mushrooms

Raw salmon

Raw tuna

Cucumber

For the sushi dipping
sauce

4 tbsp soy sauce

2 tsp wasabi paste

2 tbsp fresh ginger, finely
cut

2 tbsp rice wine vinegar

2 tbsp sesame oil

Sushi is a winner with children of all ages. It's not as difficult as you think – practice makes perfect! Just make sure you follow the instructions when cooking the rice: that's the key to successful sushi. You will need a bamboo rolling mat to do this properly.

1. Wash the rice well and drain. Cover with the measured water and bring to a simmer. Cover and cook for 12 minutes then leave to sit for 5 minutes with the lid on.
2. Meanwhile, heat the vinegar, sugar and salt until dissolved, then leave to cool.
3. Turn the cooked rice out onto a flat tray to cool. When cool, place in a bowl, stir in the vinegar solution and mix with a wooden spoon.
4. Lay half a sheet of nori seaweed onto a rolling mat. Dip your hand in cold water and quickly place a handful of rice in a line along the seaweed.
5. Flatten out with your fingertips using the water to stop any sticking. For this to work, you need to do it quickly.
6. The rice should cover half the width of the sheet, so now you can place small amounts of your different filling combinations in the middle of the rice. Whatever fillings you use, you will need to cut everything into little pieces.
7. Use the mat to roll up the sushi roll, pinch and squeeze the mat to shape it into a round cigar shape.
8. Slice into inch-thick rolls with a sharp knife, turn onto their sides so the rice is facing upwards, and serve with the pickled ginger and your sushi dipping sauce.

Sushi dipping sauce

1. Mix all the ingredients in a bowl and serve in a ramekin or dipping saucer.

105. Chicken, chorizo and herb empanadas

For the pastry

450g self-raising flour

1 tsp salt

120g butter, cold, diced

75ml cold water, to bring the dough together

For the filling

6 chicken thighs

1/2 tsp chilli powder

100g tinned tomatoes

2 chorizo sausages

1 small bunch of flat parsley, chopped

1 red pepper, diced

25g tomato purée

The basis of empanadas is pastry and there's a magic knack for making it – having nice cool hands helps. Even if they don't, kids still love creating the little empanada parcels! Plan in advance, as you need to marinate the chicken in the fridge overnight to maximise the flavour.

Pastry

1. Sieve the flour and the salt into a large bowl. Dice the butter and start to rub it into the flour.
2. Use your fingers to pick up the mixture and rub it with your thumbs until you get a texture that looks crumbly and still has little lumps of butter.
3. Gradually add the water until you get a stretchy dough. Wrap in cling film and rest in the fridge. This is important as it improves the handling quality of the pastry and makes it easier to roll out.

Filling

1. Remove the skin from the chicken thighs and place in a bag with the chilli powder and tinned tomatoes to marinate overnight.
2. The next day, remove the chicken from the bag, keeping some marinade for later.
3. If you have a BBQ or chargrill you can cook the chicken on that. Make sure you don't have too much yellow flame as this will give the food an unpleasant taste. If you don't have a BBQ place the chicken in the oven at 210°C until cooked. This will take about 30 minutes.
4. Once cooled, remove the meat from the bone and chop roughly.
5. Remove the skin from the chorizo sausage and dice.
6. Add the sausage and diced pepper to a frying pan and cook out until the sausage is cooked.
7. Add some of the marinade and the tomato purée to the pan, then add the diced chicken. Finish with the chopped parsley and cool.
8. Once cool you can start to make the empanadas. Cut your dough into four even pieces, roll the pastry out as thin as you can and then use a plain scone cutter to cut it out into circles.
9. With a pastry brush, brush one half of the cut circle with water.
10. Place a spoonful of the mix in the centre of the circle, fold over and press the edges together.
11. Continue to do this until you've used up all the pastry and mix.
12. To cook you can bake in the oven at 190°C until lightly browned or deep fry at 200°C. Both ways will take less than 10 minutes.

106. Quiche with pancetta, leek and smoked cheese

For the pastry
200g plain flour

100g butter, cold, diced

1 egg

50g Parmesan cheese, finely grated

A pinch of salt

For the filling
5 eggs, beaten

400ml double cream

150g smoky Cheddar-type cheese, grated. Isle of Mull is perfect

10 thin slices of pancetta

1/2 bunch of chives

150g leek

1 small handful of thyme tips

Salt and freshly ground black pepper

This is a tasty update on the classic Quiche Lorraine. You won't believe the difference between the flavours and textures of a homemade quiche and the cardboardy ones you might buy in a shop.

1. Preheat the oven to 190˚C.
2. Put the flour, cold butter and a pinch of salt in a bowl. Rub together with your fingertips to create a mix with a breadcrumb-like texture.
3. Add the grated Parmesan. Add the egg and bring the mix together carefully without overworking it.
4. Chill in the fridge.
5. Once your pastry has chilled, roll it out to fit a 28 cm tin with a removable bottom. See page 20 for how to line a pastry tin.
6. Line the pastry with greaseproof paper or three sheets of cling film and baking beans. Then chill again.
7. Once chilled, 'bake blind' for 10 minutes. See page 20 for how to do this.
8. Meanwhile, chop the leek and give it a good wash making sure to remove any grit and soil.
9. Cut the pancetta and pan fry until crisp, then add the leek and cook until soft.
10. Lower the oven temperature to 180˚C.
11. Mix all the other filling ingredients together, then pour the filling into the pastry case. Sprinkle over with a little extra grated cheese.
12. Bake in the oven for 30 minutes.

SWEET STUFF

Everyone loves a homemade pudding – and my guess is that some of you have bypassed every chapter in this book and come straight here. Welcome! I have been careful not to make this section too complicated. You'll find some real classics here, recipes I've been using my whole career. When I was on MasterChef, I did loads of sweet stuff. The main reason being that I had heaps of recipes to hand when I was planning my next round for the show. I'm not a pastry chef, but I love working with desserts. The science behind how this kind of cooking works fascinates me, plus the 'proof is in the pudding' aspect of watching people enjoy what you've created is very satisfying.

To take simple ingredients like flour, eggs and sugar and turn them into the most amazing delights is incredible. If you can master some of these straightforward techniques and methods, you should be able to tackle just about any sweet recipe out there. With the other recipes in this book, you have a bit of leeway in terms of quantities and being able to substitute ingredients. Here, however, the approach is more scientific and so it is vital you follow the recipes precisely.

10

107. Hazelnut shortbread

100g hazelnuts
500g plain flour
300g butter, softened
150g caster sugar
3 egg yolks
1 vanilla pod, seeds
  removed

This fabulous recipe works every time. I learned it from the amazing chef Steven Doherty during my time at Cook School Scotland.

1. Preheat the oven to 180°C.
2. Your first job is to roast and peel the hazelnuts; don't worry, it's not as difficult as it sounds. Put the nuts onto a baking tray and place in the preheated oven. Roast until the skins of the nuts turn dark brown.
3. Remove from the oven and pour into a clean tea towel. Close up the tea towel by gathering up the ends to make a little pouch. Next rub the nuts in the tea towel until all the skins have fallen off.
4. Remove the nuts from the tea towel one at a time, leaving the skins behind.
5. Now roughly chop the nuts.
6. Separate the egg yolks. Then, in a large bowl, cream the butter and sugar with your hands. Steven Doherty insisted that you always use your hands. I have tried using a spoon and can confirm it's better by hand.
7. Now add the egg yolks and vanilla seeds and work into your butter mixture. By now you'll have figured out why you need to separate the yolks before getting your hands into the mix.
8. Finally add the flour and chopped nuts and bring together to form a smooth paste.
9. Roll into sausage shapes and chill for about an hour in the fridge.
10. When you are ready to bake the shortbread cut the logs into 1 cm slices then place onto a baking tray lined with butter and flour.
11. Bake for 10 to 12 minutes at 180°C.
12. Once baked dust with a little caster sugar.

108. Apple and cinnamon scones

375g self-raising flour

65g butter, diced and cold

65g caster sugar

1/2 braeburn apple

150ml milk

A squeeze of lemon juice

1 tsp cinnamon

Milk, to finish

This recipe uses milk slightly soured with lemon juice. You might not have done this before, but it's well worth a try. Souring the milk helps the chemical reaction with the baking powder that's in the flour. This gives you a much better lift, which in turn gives you a lighter scone.

1. The first thing you need to do is to sour the milk with a squeeze of lemon juice.
2. Next, preheat the oven to 180°C.
3. Grate half an apple, including the skin.
4. Sift the flour and the cinnamon together into a large bowl.
5. Carefully rub in the cold, diced butter.
6. Add the sugar and the grated apple.
7. Add the soured milk to the mixture and knead lightly.
8. Tip out onto a floured surface and roll to a thickness of 4 to 5 cm.
9. Use a crinkled cutter and cut your scones to the size you require. You should get about a dozen scones.
10. Put on a non-stick baking sheet. I find that if you bunch them relatively close together you get a better lift. Then brush with milk and cook for about 10 to 16 minutes depending on size.

109. Chocolate chip cookies

140g soft dark brown sugar

60g butter

1 egg, beaten

40g porridge oats

50g desiccated coconut, fine

1/2 tsp of vanilla essence

75g plain chocolate chips

140g self-raising flour

Pinch of salt

Silicon paper to line your baking tray

The chocolate chip cookie is an easy thing to make but a tricky thing to get right – everyone has their own take on how squidgy, gooey, crunchy, fudgy they should be. I love this recipe for the fact that the chocolate is plain, not milk, and the addition of the porridge and the coconut gives the cookies a brilliant chewy texture.

1. Preheat your oven to 160°C.
2. Mix the salt, flour, coconut and oats together in a bowl.
3. Now cream the butter and sugar together. I find it's much easier to do this with your hands. (If you're interested, I explain the reason for this on page 221!)
4. Add the beaten egg and vanilla essence, and next the chocolate chips.
5. You should now have a lovely dough which you can roll out to 5 mm thick.
6. Use a 7.5 cm plain cutter to cut out the cookies. You should get about 20 cookies.
7. Bake them in the oven on a tray lined with silicon paper at 160°C for 10 minutes.
8. Allow to cool on a wire rack.

110. Pistachio biscotti

135g granulated white sugar

2 eggs

1 tsp vanilla extract or vanilla seeds from a pod

1 tsp baking powder

230g plain flour

60g pistachio nuts, coarsely chopped

Pinch of salt

These are biscotti to fall in love with. They are twice-baked and because you've made them at home, you'll find they have a much nicer texture than shop-bought ones.

1. Preheat the oven to 175°C.
2. Line a baking sheet by rubbing cold butter onto it and then dusting with flour.
3. In a bowl, beat the sugar and eggs until thick, pale and fluffy.
4. Next add in the vanilla extract or seeds from a split vanilla pod.
5. In a separate bowl, whisk together the flour, baking powder and salt.
6. Add this to the egg mixture and beat until combined.
7. Fold in the chopped pistachio nuts.
8. Transfer the dough to a well-floured surface and roll into a log shape, about 30 cm long and 8 cm wide.
9. You may have to flour your hands to form the log, as the dough will be quite sticky.
10. Place the log on the baking sheet and bake for about 25 minutes or until firm to the touch.
11. Remove from the oven, reduce oven temperature to 150°C and let the log cool on a wire rack for about 10 minutes.
12. Now transfer the log to a cutting board and cut into about 1.5 cm slices.
13. Place the biscotti, cut side down, on the baking sheet.
14. Bake for another 8 to 10 minutes, turn slices over, and bake for 8 to 10 minutes more or until golden brown.
15. Remove from the oven and allow to cool.

111. **Summer strawberries** with passion fruit, lime and vanilla syrup

500g fresh strawberries
300g fresh blueberries
3 passion fruits
75g sugar
1 lime
1 vanilla pod

This simple, delicate dish features strawberries perfectly in season. When you prepare strawberries always wash them before cutting off the stalk. The reason is that the strawberry is waterproof up until you cut into it. If you wash the fruit after you've cut it, it will just absorb water and go mushy.

1. Your first job is to make the passion fruit, lime and vanilla syrup.
2. To do this, halve and scoop the pulp from the passion fruit into a small pot, then split the vanilla pod in half lengthwise and scoop out the seeds and add to the passion fruit.
3. Next, use a peeler to remove the peel from the lime; then with a knife carefully remove the white pith from the skin.
4. Cut the skin into very thin strips and add to the passion fruit and vanilla. Next add the sugar.
5. Now halve the lime and squeeze the juice into the pot. If you microwave the lime for a few seconds first you get much more juice from it.
6. Pop onto the stove and bring to the boil. Once your syrup is boiled remove it from the heat.
7. Now prepare your strawberries, rinse your blueberries and, last of all, pour the syrup over the fruit about 20 minutes before you'd like to serve.

112. Summer pudding

Strawberries, 1 punnet
Blackberries, 1 punnet
Redcurrants, 1 punnet
Raspberries, 1 punnet
150g caster sugar
1 vanilla pod, split
8 slices white bread,
  square plain bread is
  best
Clotted cream, to serve

This traditional pudding is a joy to make in the summer months when all its fruits are in season. It is so easy and always a particular hit with little kids. Remember to plan in advance – you need to put the puddings in the fridge overnight. This gives the fruit a chance to soak into the bread and creates a wonderful bright red finish.

1. Your first job is to prepare the fruit. Wash all the fruit before cutting so it doesn't become soggy.
2. Hull the strawberries and halve the raspberries, then remove the hulls from the blackberries and take the redcurrants off the stalk.
3. Pop about two thirds of the fruit into a pan with the sugar and the seeds from the split vanilla pod. Then add 50ml of water and pop on the stove.
4. Heat the fruit until the sugar melts and the fruit starts to bleed. Be very careful at this stage that you don't overheat the fruit, especially when the fruit is in season as it's much softer.
5. Remove the pan from the heat and add the third of fruit you kept aside; allow to cool.
6. The next task is to line the pudding basin or basins. I like to make four little individual ones, but it's up to you. First, take some cling film and lay sheets onto your work surface. You will probably need about three layers.
7. Pop a little water into the bottom of each pudding basin, then push your cling film into the basin. You'll find that the water helps hold the film in place.
8. Next take your bread, cut the crusts off and very lightly pin the bread out a little with a rolling pin.
9. Now cut out your bases – use the pudding basin as a guide, but remember the base of your pudding is the size of the open top of the basin.
10. Shape the bread for the sides. If you are using a large bowl you won't need to do much trimming. If they are smaller cut the bread in half.
11. Now start to build the layers of bread into the basin. Press each layer onto the next one until the sides are completely covered.
12. Spoon in the fruit mixture, pressing down gently with each spoonful.
13. Once you have filled each basin with fruit fold over any excess bread and top with the base you cut earlier.
14. Pull up the excess cling film and tighten by twisting the film.
15. Place the puddings into the fridge overnight.
16. When ready, serve with clotted cream and any fruit mix left over.

113. Coconut panna cotta with pineapple compote

For the panna cotta

4 x 11 cm sheets of gelatine, soaked in cold water

400ml tin of coconut milk

40g caster sugar

60ml double cream

1 vanilla pod, split and seeds removed

30g desiccated coconut

For the compote

1/2 pineapple, finely diced or sliced

1/2 red chilli, finely diced

20g root ginger, finely diced

50g sugar

1 tbsp water

Not many puddings are as refreshing as this one. The coconutty creaminess balanced out by the tanginess of the compote – with its neat chilli kick – creates a panna cotta to die for.

Panna cotta

1. Soak the gelatine in ice-cold water until soft. This should take about 10 minutes. Use a bowl big enough to place the full sheet into the water without having to break or fold the gelatine.
2. Bring the cream, coconut milk and vanilla seeds gently to the boil.
3. Once boiling take off the heat, add the sugar and allow to infuse for 5 to 10 minutes.
4. Now add the gelatine. Make sure you squeeze out the water; the gelatine should be soft but intact.
5. Allow the mixture to cool slightly and then pour into serving moulds, either four little ones or one larger one. Put in the fridge and chill.
6. Meanwhile, carefully toast the coconut in the oven for between 5 and 10 minutes.
7. Once the coconut is cool and the panna cotta is set, sprinkle the coconut on top.

Pineapple compote

1. Place the sugar, water, ginger and chilli into a pot and bring this mixture to the boil.
2. Once boiled add the pineapple and remove from the heat.
3. Cool and refrigerate before serving.

114. Chocolate and orange mousse
with candy peel

For the candy peel
2 oranges
150g granulated sugar
100g caster sugar
100ml water

For the mousse
100g granulated sugar
100ml water
3 eggs, yolks only
1 orange, zest grated
175g dark chocolate,
  53% cocoa or above
1 x 11 cm gelatine sheet,
  soaked in ice-cold water
250g double cream,
  whipped

To finish
Fresh orange slices

This mousse is a wee show stopper. It's mouth-wateringly good on its own, but I love the curls of homemade candy peel which lift this dessert to new heights. Plan a little in advance as the peel takes a few hours to dry out.

Candy peel
1. Give the oranges a good wash and then, using a potato peeler, peel the skin of the orange from top to bottom.
2. Remove any white pith and then cut the orange skin into thin strips.
3. Pop the strips of peel in a pan and cover with cold water.
4. Bring to a boil, drain the water and then repeat this process twice more.
5. Meanwhile peel and segment the oranges and put the segments to one side until needed.
6. In a small pan add the granulated sugar and water and bring to a simmer. Let the mixture cook for 7 to 8 minutes at a constant simmer.
7. Add the peel and cook until the peels are translucent. Adjust the heat as necessary so as not to overheat the sugar.
8. Avoid stirring; instead, use a small pastry brush to brush down any sugar that starts to form around the pan as this will help prevent crystallisation.
9. Once the peels are translucent remove from the syrup and drain. Pop them into a bowl with the caster sugar so that you can coat each strand.
10. Remove the peels and spread them out on a drying rack and leave to dry for 4 to 5 hours.

Mousse
1. Boil the sugar and water to make a stock syrup. You will need 65g of syrup for this recipe.
2. Place the yolks into the bowl of a food mixer and whisk until light and almost white.
3. Pour over 65g of boiling sugar syrup and whisk until thick.
4. Add the grated orange zest and remove from the mixer.
5. Meanwhile melt the chocolate in a bowl over some warm water.
6. Add the melted chocolate into the egg yolk and sugar mix and fold in quickly.
7. Drain the gelatine out of the ice-cold water (see page 233 for how to do this), melt it in the microwave and fold it into the foamy chocolate-egg mixture, which is called a sabayon.
8. Carefully fold in the whipped cream.
9. Place into prepared glasses and top with fresh orange and candy peel.

115. Chocolate and hazelnut cheesecake

150g cream cheese

175g Mascarpone cheese

350ml double cream

200g dark chocolate

250g biscuits, digestives are a classic for this

100g butter, melted

100g hazelnuts

Seasonal berries to serve

Rich and decadent, this is a stunning no-bake cheesecake. You can use a classic digestive biscuit to make the base, but there are plenty who swear by Lotus biscoff as a cheescake base; they're those caramel-tasting biscuits you get at the side of your latte in cafés the world over.

1. Preheat your oven to 180°C.
2. Your first job is to make the hazelnut and chocolate ganache. To do this, pop the hazelnuts onto a tray and put in the oven to roast. Roasting the hazelnuts helps skin them and brings out the most amazing flavour of the nuts.
3. Roast until golden brown. Then pour the nuts into a clean tea towel, pull up the sides to create a pouch and then rub the hazelnuts until the skins fall off.
4. Crush the nuts in a food processor or with a rolling pin. Don't break them down too much as having a little crunch in the cheesecake is brilliant.
5. Break the chocolate into small pieces and pop into a bowl.
6. Bring 200ml of the double cream to the boil and pour it over the chocolate, add the crushed nuts and mix. Put to one side.
7. Crush the biscuits, either in a food processor or in a bag with a rolling pin. Again, leave a little texture – stop when you get a nice crumbly consistency.
8. Next mix the melted butter into the biscuit crumb.
9. Add the biscuit and butter mixture to a cake tin or mousse rings. Push the mix down with the back of a spoon until it has compressed together.
10. Leave to set in the fridge for 30 minutes.
11. Mix the cream cheese and the Mascarpone cheese together with a whisk, add the remaining double cream and whisk some more.
12. Finally fold through the melted chocolate and nuts mixture. The plan is to try not to mix too much – I always think the marbled effect looks great.
13. Spoon the mixture over the cooled biscuit base and leave in the fridge to set for a couple of hours.
14. This cheesecake tastes amazing served with fresh, seasonal berries.

116. Baked vanilla cheesecake with cherry compote

A classic baked cheesecake never disappoints! The tart cherry compote – with its hint of booziness – makes this one a delicious, sure-fire winner.

For the cheescake

250g biscuits, digestives are great but you choose

125g butter, melted

600g cream cheese

2 tbsp plain flour

175g sugar

1 tsp vanilla essence

2 eggs, beaten

1 egg yolk, beaten

140g double cream

For the compote

200g fresh cherries

50g caster sugar

30ml cherry liquor

Cheesecake

1. Preheat your oven to 180°C.
2. Crush the biscuits in a bag with a rolling pin, then mix with the melted butter.
3. Press into a 20 cm spring-form ring or individual rings and bake for 5 minutes.
4. Then, for the cheesecake mix, beat the cream cheese with the flour, sugar, vanilla essence, eggs and cream. Pour into your tins.
5. Bake for 12 to 15 minutes if you are using individual rings, or about 40 minutes if you are baking in a bigger spring-form ring.
6. Check before you take it out of the oven – the cheesecake should be slightly wobbly in the centre.
7. Allow to cool before cutting and serving with the cold compote.

For the compote

1. If you have a cherry stoner, use it then cut the cherries in half. If not use a small knife to cut the cherries in half. You will need to work around the stone a little until it's halved and then remove the stone and the stalk.
2. Place the cherries with the sugar into a small pan and heat up. Try to keep the cherries moving in the pan until the sugar starts to melt.
3. Once the sugar has melted and the cherries have a nice glaze, add the liquor. Be careful as it will flambé – this is fun but only if you know it's going to happen!

117. Baked rice pudding with hazelnuts and honey

50g risotto or pudding
  rice
550ml full fat milk
30g caster sugar
1 tsp vanilla extract
30g honey
100g hazelnuts

Rice pudding has something of a bad reputation that's not entirely warranted. Made properly – with milk not cream, and with the addition of some 21st-century touches of flavour – it can be one of the most exquisite, comforting puddings imaginable. Think about your timings with this recipe, as it involves leaving the pudding to rest for an hour after cooking so the lovely creamy texture can develop.

1. Preheat the oven to 150°C.
2. Roast the hazelnuts in the oven for about 7 to 8 minutes.
3. When you remove them from the oven, pour them into a clean tea towel, make a little pouch with the cloth and rub the hazelnuts together until the skin rubs off.
4. Next roughly chop the nuts and put to one side.
5. You might be wondering how 50 grams of rice to 550ml of milk can work, but trust me it will – please don't be tempted to add more milk.
6. Rinse the rice in cold water to remove the dusty starch from the surface – this prevents the pudding becoming too thick.
7. Place the drained rice in a large saucepan with the milk, vanilla extract and sugar.
8. Bring to the boil then turn the heat down and simmer very gently, stirring every few minutes, for 15 minutes.
9. Simmer for five more minutes, stirring slowly all the time to prevent the rice from sticking to the bottom of the pan.
10. Remove from the heat and add 75g of the chopped hazelnuts.
11. Pour into a shallow ovenproof dish.
12. Bake in the oven for 30 minutes and then leave to rest for at least one hour.
13. Scatter with the remainder of the nuts and drizzle the honey over the top.

118. Tiramisu

500ml double cream
300g Mascarpone cheese
50g icing sugar
50g instant coffee
100ml water
100ml Tia Maria
1 pack of sponge fingers
1 bar of dark chocolate
Cocoa powder, to dust

You might think of tiramisu as a stalwart of the Italian pudding repertoire, but in fact it's a relatively recent invention of the past 50 years. It's super simple and when done well is absolutely delightful. Make it a little in advance so all the flavours can mingle nicely.

1. Sieve the icing sugar into a bowl, add the cream and whisk to soft peaks.
2. In a separate bowl, whisk the Mascarpone cheese until soft and then fold both mixes together.
3. Heat 100ml of water and stir in the instant coffee.
4. Now mix the coffee and the Tia Maria together.
5. Soak the sponge fingers one at a time in the coffee and alcohol mix.
6. Then place a row of sponge fingers in the bottom of your dish and add a layer of cheese and cream mix.
7. Dust with cocoa powder.
8. Continue layering the sponge fingers, cream mix and cocoa until the dish is filled.
9. Top with grated chocolate and chill in the fridge until ready to serve.

119. Chocolate brownies with cherry and walnut

250g chocolate, 70% cocoa
250g butter
300g caster sugar
3 eggs
1 egg yolk, lightly beaten
60g plain flour, sifted
1/2 tsp baking powder
60g cocoa powder
100g walnuts, optional
100g dried sour cherries
Pinch of salt

These indulgent brownies have just the right amount of squidge. You can leave out the walnuts if you like but please not the cherries – they're the perfect complement to the rich, dark chocolate.

1. Preheat the oven to 180°C, and line a 23 cm x 23 cm baking tin with baking parchment.
2. Set a bowl over, but not touching, a pan of simmering water, and add 200g of the chocolate, broken into pieces. Allow to melt, stirring occasionally, then remove from the heat immediately.
3. Meanwhile, beat the butter and sugar together in a food processor until light and fluffy, and break the rest of the chocolate into chips.
4. With the mixer still running, gradually add the eggs and the egg yolk, beating well between each addition to ensure they're thoroughly incorporated before pouring in any more. Leave mixing on a high speed for five minutes until the mix has a silky sheen, and has increased in volume.
5. Remove the bowl from the mixer, and gently fold in the melted chocolate and chocolate chips with a metal spoon, followed by the flour, baking powder, salt, cocoa powder, walnuts and sour cherries.
6. Spoon the mixture into the tin, and bake for 30 minutes. Test with a metal skewer; it should come out sticky, but not coated with raw mixture.
7. If it does, put it back into the oven for another 3 minutes, then test again.
8. When the brownies are ready, remove the tin from the oven.
9. Leave to cool for an hour before cutting into squares.

120. Victoria sponge

For the sponge
225g butter, softened at room temperature
225g caster sugar
4 eggs
2 tsp vanilla extract
225g self-raising flour
Milk, to mix
Icing sugar, to dust

For the filling
250g double cream
1 tsp vanilla extract
40g sugar
150g jam of your choice
50g icing sugar

For lots of us, a Victoria sponge feels like the quintessential cake. There's something about its simplicity and lack of fuss that makes it really appealing – it's perfect for an afternoon tea or a children's birthday party.

Sponge
1. Preheat the oven to 180°C.
2. Grease and line 2 x 18 cm cake tins with baking paper.
3. Cream the butter and the sugar together in a bowl until pale and fluffy.
4. Beat in the eggs, a little at a time, and stir in the vanilla extract.
5. Fold in the flour using a large metal spoon, adding a little extra milk if necessary. You want to create a batter with a soft dropping consistency.
6. Divide the mixture between the cake tins and gently spread out with a spatula.
7. Bake for 20 to 25 minutes, or until golden-brown on top and a skewer inserted into the middle comes out clean.
8. Remove from the oven and set aside for 5 minutes, then remove from the tin and peel off the paper.
9. Place onto a wire rack to cool.

Filling
1. Place the double cream, sugars and vanilla extract into a bowl and whisk until the cream is whipped into fluffy peaks.
2. In a small bowl mix the jam until it's spreadable, upturn the two sponges and spread the jam onto them. Make sure you keep the best-looking sponge for the top.
3. Next spread or pipe the cream onto the bottom layer and then carefully place the other sponge on top.
4. Before serving dust with icing sugar.

121. Carrot cake

For the cake

4 eggs

300ml vegetable oil

200g caster sugar

200g light soft brown sugar

2 tsp vanilla extract

250g plain flour

2 tsp bicarbonate of soda

2 tsp baking powder

1/2 tsp salt

2 tsp ground cinnamon

350g carrots, grated

125g walnuts, chopped

For the icing and filling

125g butter, softened

200g cream cheese, softened

125g icing sugar

1 tsp vanilla extract

125g walnuts, chopped

I don't know who first created carrot cake, but the addition of such a humble vegetable to a cake was a small act of genius. The carrots give a real moistness to the cake, and the cream cheese frosting certainly stops it feeling too healthy!

1. Preheat the oven to 175°C.
2. Grease and flour two 20 cm baking tins.
3. In a large bowl, beat together the eggs, oil, both the sugars and the vanilla extract.
4. Next, sift the flour, bicarbonate of soda, baking powder, salt and cinnamon, and mix in.
5. Stir in the carrots and fold in the walnuts.
6. Divide the mixture between the prepared tins.
7. Bake in the preheated oven for 40 to 50 minutes or until a skewer inserted into the centre of the cake comes out clean.
8. Let the cakes cool in the tins for 10 minutes, then turn them out onto a wire rack to cool completely.
9. Now you need to make the topping and filling.
10. Combine the butter, cream cheese, icing sugar and vanilla extract, then beat until the mixture is smooth and creamy.
11. Use half the icing to sandwich the two cakes together and then spread the other half over the top of cake when it has cooled and decorate with chopped nuts if you wish.

122. Red berry pavlova

For the pavlova
4 egg whites
250g caster sugar
2 tsp cornflour
1 tsp vinegar
1 drop of vanilla extract
A pinch of salt

For the filling
300ml double cream
30g caster sugar
1 vanilla pod
300g red berries of your
  choice, to finish

Fantastic and fun, this recipe is a great way of using up egg whites. It'll be easier if you have a mixing machine or a hand-held electric whisk, but there are always two rules to follow when making pavlova.

- All equipment must be spotlessly clean. If fat traces get in, they will stop the egg whites from holding. You'll have a pavlova fail on your hands!

- The whites must be free from blood spots and yolk, and will work best at room temperature.

1. Preheat your oven to 100˚C.
2. Place the egg whites in a large clean bowl with a pinch of salt.
3. Whisk the whites until they have become stiff peaks, then add the vinegar and the vanilla extract to the whites.
4. Mix the cornflour with the sugar and, in a continuous stream, whisk this mixture into the stiff whites. You should now have a very white, light mix. If you feel brave you could do the 'meringue test'. Hold the bowl over your head and if the mix stays in the bowl it's perfect!
5. You now have a number of different ways of shaping this mix. You could pipe into traditional nests or rosettes or you could lightly oil a scone cutter, fill it with the mixture and then remove the cutter, leaving you with a uniform shape. Or, you could take two spoons and 'quenelle' the mixture into little torpedo shapes. What ever you decide, it will look great. Here, I have opted for a gateau-style pavlova.
6. Cut some greaseproof paper to the shape of your tray. Place a little spot of the meringue mix onto each corner of the tray before putting the paper on top. This will hold the paper onto the tray, which is especially handy if you have a fan-assisted oven as it stops the paper blowing onto the meringue.
7. Once you have your meringue shapes, place your tray into the oven for 70 minutes or so, depending on the size of the pavlova and how soft you like the centre. Either way, it should come out of the oven perfectly white and light.
8. To finish, split the vanilla pod lengthwise. It's much easier to split if you run the back of a knife along the pod to flatten it out. Once you have split the pod scrape out the seeds and put them in a bowl with the double cream and sugar.
9. Whip the cream, sugar and vanilla together until you get soft peaks.
10. You are now ready to build your dessert. Remember that the great thing about pavlova is you can have any kind you like; all you need is a little imagination. You can have very artistic, professional-looking ones for dinner parties and fun bright ones for kids. The only difference is the filling and the shape – so have some fun!

123. Lemon meringue tart

For the sweet pastry

200g plain flour

125g butter, chilled

1 egg

50g sugar

1 pinch of salt

For the lemon curd filling

2 egg yolks

100g caster sugar

100g butter

1 lemon, juiced and zested

For the Italian meringue

4 egg whites, at room temperature

200g caster sugar

60ml water

1/2 lemon, juiced

A cook's thermometer is useful

This dish takes skill, but I remember making it in home economics when I was 13 and getting a result. Perhaps the only subject I can claim a result in, but that's another story. Everyone loves lemon meringue tart, and all your hard work is worth it when you taste the sweet caramelised meringue, zingy lemon filling and crisp pastry. It's my wife Sharon's favourite: she still fondly remembers the one she ate at our first anniversary dinner. Unfortunately I didn't make it and I've been trying to live up to it ever since.

Sweet pastry

1. Sieve the flour and the salt into a bowl.
2. Dice the chilled butter and add to the flour, then lightly rub in the butter to achieve a sandy texture. Do this by running your hands down the insides of the bowl and go right to the bottom, when your fingers meet slowly lift them out or the bowl rubbing your thumbs over your fingers as you go.
3. The secret of perfect pastry is to make sure you don't work it too much at this stage. I always try and make sure I don't rub all the butter in completely. Even when I have finished rubbing in, I still like to see little flakes of butter.
4. Mix the egg and the sugar together. Make a well in the centre of the flour and butter, and add the sugar and the egg mixture.
5. Gradually incorporate into the flour and carefully bring together until you have a smooth paste.
6. Press into a flat round, wrap in cling film and allow to rest in the fridge for an hour before using. The reason you press the pastry into a flat round is so that you can pin it straight from the fridge.
7. You will need to roll out the pastry to line your tin. And then you will need to blind bake your pastry case. See page 20 for how to do this.

Lemon curd filling

1. In a large bowl whisk the egg yolks until they start to turn white.
2. Now add the sugar, butter, lemon juice and lemon zest.
3. Next you will need to cook the mixture until it becomes thick. To do this you need a pan that holds the bowl securely. Put a little water in the bottom of the pan, place it on the heat and bring to a simmer.
4. Now put the bowl with your egg yolk mix over the water and whisk until the mixture thickens. This will take about 25 minutes, but the end result is worth it.
5. You can make this the day before and keep it in the fridge overnight.

continues on the next page

123. Lemon meringue tart

Italian meringue

1. Italian meringue is different to French meringue in that the sugar is turned into a hot syrup before being added to the egg whites. Why? Because the hot syrup cooks the egg white. This allows you to use it in quick cook recipes like lemon meringue pie and baked Alaska.

2. However, the same rules apply as to French meringue. Make sure all your equipment is spotless. Any trace of fat can ruin your meringue.

3. Pour your sugar and water into a small pan. Slowly and carefully mix the sugar and water together making sure the sugar has dissolved.

4. At this stage I take a pastry brush and brush down the sides of the pan with a little water. This gets the sugar crystals off the side of the pan and reduces the risk of crystallisation.

5. Place the pan on a low heat.

6. Place the egg whites into a large clean bowl. Now switch the whisk on to a slow speed and whisk for 3 to 4 minutes.

7. Add a squeeze of lemon juice – this helps strengthen the whites.

8. Increase the speed on the whisk to medium for 1 minute, or until the whites start to take in air and show signs of doubling in volume.

9. Now whisk at the highest speed and continue whisking through the soft peak stage until stiff peaks are formed. The whites should be all cloudy and foamy at this stage. Make sure they are nice and stiff before you add the sugar syrup.

10. Once the sugar syrup reaches 121°C, start to add it to the egg whites.

11. Whisk the sugar into the mixture on a fast speed, then slowly pour the hot sugar into the mix until you have a stiff, glossy mixture with a satin sheen. Whisk until the mixture has cooled down.

12. This mixture is great for loads of different desserts. You can even pipe it straight onto the plate and blow torch or grill it.

To finish

1. Preheat the grill.

2. Spread the lemon curd onto your baked and cooled pastry case.

3. You now have a couple of options for adding the meringue. You can pipe it on with a star nozzle, do the spiky thing so it looks the same as you buy in the shops, or you could simply spread it over the top.

4. Your last job is to caramelise the meringue. I find the best way is under the grill, but most chefs blowtorch it as it's quicker and there's less chance of burning it. If you are grilling, make sure you keep the tart as far from the heat as possible and never take your eyes off it.

124. Sticky toffee pudding with honey glazed figs and cinnamon ricotta cheese

55g butter, plus extra for greasing

170g Demerara sugar

1 tbsp golden syrup

2 eggs

2 tbsp black treacle

200g self-raising flour, plus extra for dusting

200g dates, pitted

290ml water, boiling

1 tsp bicarbonate of soda

1/2 tsp vanilla extract

For the glazed figs

6 figs, fresh

2 tbsp honey

For the ricotta cheese

200g ricotta cheese

1 tbsp honey

Cinnamon, a pinch

For the sauce

110ml double cream

55g butter, diced

55g dark muscovado sugar

2 tbsp black treacle

1 tbsp golden syrup

You will need five or six little pudding moulds to make these gorgeous individual twists on the ultimate classic pudding. The honeyed figgy extra makes them more irresistible than ever.

1. Preheat the oven to 180°C.
2. Brush the sides of your pudding moulds with butter and then dust in some flour; this will stop the puddings sticking to the moulds.
3. Cream the butter and sugar together in a mixer until pale and fluffy.
4. Mix together the golden syrup, treacle and eggs, then add them a little at a time to the butter and sugar mix, and blend until smooth.
5. Now add the flour and blend, at a low speed, until well combined. Transfer to a clean bowl.
6. Meanwhile, blend the dates and boiling water in a food processor to a smooth purée.
7. Stir in the bicarbonate of soda and vanilla extract.
8. Pour the date purée into the pudding batter and stir until well combined.
9. Pour the mixture into the moulds and bake for 20 to 25 minutes, or until the top is springy and golden-brown.
10. Meanwhile cut your figs in half through the middle and drizzle with the honey. Then pop under a hot grill for a few moments or carefully pan fry in a dry pan.
11. Now mix the honey with the ricotta and the cinnamon.
12. To make the sauce, heat all of the ingredients in a pan, stirring occasionally, until boiling.
13. Serve the puddings with a honeyed fig on top, plus the ricotta cheese and lashings of the hot sauce.

125. Crème brûlée

565ml double cream
100g caster sugar
1 vanilla pod
6 egg yolks
A sprinkle of caster sugar, to finish

Crunchy and custardy with a distinctive burnt caramel flavour, these puddings are little pots of decadent delight. Here are two ways to create a dinner party classic.

Method one

1. Preheat your oven to 150°C.
2. Split the vanilla pod lengthwise and place into a thick-bottomed pot with the cream and slowly heat up.
3. Whisk the egg yolks and sugar together until the yolks lighten.
4. Now add half of the warm cream to the egg yolk mix stirring with a wire whisk as you go, and then pour this mixture into the rest of the cream.
5. Place in little ramekins or a dish and then put onto a shallow tray. If your're using little dishes, you'll need about six for this recipe.
6. Carefully fill the tray with water.
7. Place the tray into the oven for 30 to 40 minutes until the puddings have set.
8. Once cool, put into the fridge until needed.
9. To create the topping, sprinkle a thin layer of caster sugar on top of the set brûlée. You now have a couple of options on how to melt it. I like to use a blowtorch. Or you can use a brûlée iron if you have one or place under a very hot grill.

Method two

1. Split the vanilla pod lengthwise and place into a thick-bottomed pot with the cream and slowly heat up.
2. Whisk the egg yolks and sugar together until the yolks lighten.
3. As the cream comes to the boil add half the boiling cream to the egg yolk mix. Then pour this mixture into the rest of the cream and put back onto the stove.
4. You now have to be very careful. Keep stirring the mix until it starts to thicken. You will notice it start to resemble thin custard.
5. Once it coats the back of the spoon pour the mixture into a large jug or bowl. This instantly stops the cooking.
6. Pour this mixture into your ramekins or dish. Once it's cool put into the fridge to set.
7. To glaze see step 9 above.

126. Bakewell tart

For the sweet pastry
200g plain flour
125g butter
1 egg
50g sugar
1 pinch of salt

For the sponge and to finish
100g butter
100g sugar
100g almonds, ground
2 eggs, beaten
10g plain flour
50g raspberry jam
50g apricot jam, gently warmed
A little egg, to finish

A true Bakewell tart has crisp sweet pastry, a lovely layer of jam and a heavenly frangipane filling.

Sweet pastry

1. Sieve the flour and the salt into a bowl.
2. Dice the butter and add to the flour. Now lightly rub in the butter to achieve a sandy texture. I try not to rub the butter in completely – it's good to still see little flakes of butter once you've finished rubbing in.
3. Mix the egg and the sugar together. Make a well in the centre of the flour and butter and add the sugar and the egg mixture.
4. Gradually incorporate into the flour and carefully bring together until you have a smooth paste. Less is more at this stage. The secret of perfect pastry is to make sure you don't overwork it.
5. Press into a flat round shape, wrap in cling film and allow to rest in the fridge for an hour before using. The reason you press it into a flat round is so you can pin the pastry straight from the fridge.

Sponge and to finish

1. Cream the butter and the sugar together, then gradually beat in the eggs.
2. Mix in the ground almonds and the flour.
3. When your pastry is rested, line your flan ring using three quarters of it.
4. You don't need to bake the pastry first, but you do need to pierce the bottom a few times with a fork.
5. Now spread the pastry with the raspberry jam and then with the almond sponge mix.
6. Roll the remaining pastry and cut into ½ cm strips and then arrange them in a neat criss-cross pattern on top of the almond sponge mixture.
7. Brush with a little egg wash and bake in the oven at 180°C for 30 to 40 minutes.
8. Once cooked brush with the hot apricot jam.

127. Chocolate tart

For the sweet pastry
200g plain flour
125g butter
1 egg
50g sugar
1 pinch of salt

For the filling
250g plain chocolate
100ml milk
175ml double cream
2 eggs

This gorgeously rich tart is a brilliant dessert to make ahead for a dinner party.

1. First you will need to make your sweet pastry. For how to do this, see my recipe for lemon meringue tart on page 251.
2. Now you need to line a 20 cm x 2 cm tart case with your pastry, and then bake it blind. To learn how to do this, read the section on pastry skills on page 20.
3. Preheat the oven to 180°C – this is very important as you will see later.
4. In a bowl whisk the eggs until they turn a light yellow colour.
5. Now melt the chocolate. The best way to do this is to place the chocolate into a bowl, put a little water into a pot and place the bowl on top of the pot of water.
6. Place the pot onto a low heat on the stove. Do not allow the water to boil as the steam this creates will be too hot for the chocolate.
7. Heat the milk and cream together, but do not boil.
8. Pour onto the whisked eggs and then pass this through a fine strainer onto the chocolate and mix quickly.
9. Fill your sweet pasty case with the chocolate filling.
10. Put the tart into the preheated oven and then turn the oven off immediately.
11. You need to leave the tart in the oven for 45 minutes – trust me, there will be enough residual heat to set the tart.
12. Then remove and allow the chocolate tart to cool to room temperature before cutting.

128. Baked lemon tart

For the sweet pastry
200g plain flour

125g butter

1 egg

50g sugar

1 pinch of salt

For the filling
2 large lemons, zest and juice

150g double cream

195g caster sugar

4 eggs

1 egg yolk

A cook's thermometer is useful, if you have one

This traditional French tart is all about the citrus – with a nice crisp pastry, the filling should stand out as smooth and exquisitely lemony.

1. First you will need to make your sweet pastry. For how to do this, see my recipe for lemon meringue tart on page 251.
2. Now you need to line a 20 cm x 2 cm tart case with your pastry, and then bake it blind. To learn how to do this, read the section on pastry skills on page 20.
3. Now preheat the oven to 120°C.
4. Put all the ingredients for your lemon filling in a bowl and mix together.
5. Place the bowl over a saucepan of simmering water and allow to warm up to 62°C. Make sure you continually stir the mixture and check that the water isn't touching the bowl or boiling.
6. When it reaches 62°C strain the mixture through a fine sieve into a jug.
7. Pour the mixture into the pastry case and bake for about 25 minutes.
8. To check if the tart is set, give the tray a little shoogle: if there's no movement it's ready.

SERVICE!

Well, what's this chapter about? The plan is to ensure that the chef doesn't endure hours handcuffed to the oven.

When I was a young guy I would invite friends and family over for dinner, then spend days pulling the thing together, working nonstop the whole time my guests were over. By the time I actually got to sit down, everyone was ready to go home. I think every keen cook goes through this; you are so focused on making sure you show off your new skills and dishes to your friends that you forget why your friends and family are over in the first place. The answer is: to see you! I have learned that the most important thing about having a gathering is that you are actually present. Now I never spend the night in the kitchen when I invite people over.

Just a little footnote, chefs never ever get invited over for dinner. People are scared to cook for chefs. I am not sure why: we are the easiest bunch to cater for as we fully understand the work involved and appreciate someone cooking for us. If you have a friend or family member who is a chef then get them round for dinner; I promise you they will be over the moon and they will never criticise or critique.

11

How to entertain: my top ten tips

My thoughts on home entertaining have changed over the years. I once thought it was all about the food: showcasing skills and providing restaurant-style and quality meals. Which is almost impossible at home. For me now, it's all about the people. I have learned much more by doing it wrong than doing it right. So here are my tips on how to survive, and enjoy, entertaining at home.

1. **Plan, plan and plan again.** I know it's boring, but it's vital. Plan what you are going to serve, plan when you are going to prepare it and plan how you are going to deliver it.

2. **Do not serve food on individual plates.** This one is just as important as planning. But do serve it on platters, bowls or large plates, which you can place on the dining table. There are two reasons for this. One: if you serve in bulk it's much easier to deliver food hot and in perfect condition. Two: your guests can help themselves. This not only saves you a load of stress but also makes for a much more pleasant dining experience for your guests. They won't feel obliged to eat a plate full that you have given them and they can pick and choose what they want to eat. I also find kids large and small eat more food this way. They start off being a little apprehensive, but before long they are back up for seconds. This style of serving food is rightly enough called 'Family Service'.

3. **Cook for your actual guests** and style the food accordingly. By which I mean: think about the age group, personalities and occasion. Ask yourself what you would expect if you were going to this event. A night with the boss for dinner is very different from a crowd of your closest friends.

4. **Think about the equipment you have in your kitchen** and design your menu carefully, taking this into account. Try and have a good mix of food coming from every area of the kitchen – some things from the oven, some done in the pressure cooker if you have one, some from the stove. Also ensure you have cold food on your menu as this also uses that vital bit of kit – the fridge. Try not to have too much food coming from the same place.

5. **Recruit some assistants,** even if you are a kitchen maverick who always cooks alone. Sorting the table, setting cutlery and glasses – help with these can be a real time saver for you. Even if your assistants haven't got a clue about what's needing done in a kitchen, I'm sure they can sort out tableware!

6. **Work within your capabilities** and don't be over ambitious. Don't create a whole dinner entirely with new recipes: always have a couple of dishes that you know inside out. This will give you the headspace and time to try something different. It also ensures your guests have something edible to eat if the new stuff doesn't work out!

7. **Minimum work and maximum impact.** Think of what you can buy that involves very little work but provides a proper wow factor. The big flavours of smoked products are brilliant crowd pleasers. For example, hot and cold smoked salmon, duck breast or smoked chicken all take little work to make your own. Cured meats, pickled vegetables and olives make impactful intermediate courses.

8. **Practise if you can,** especially if you want to try something different. Chefs always practise new dishes long before they attempt to serve them to the public.

9. **Taste, taste and taste again.** It's vital to taste food when you cook. For most chefs this is pure instinct. As I said at the start, it's like driving a car: to change gear you press the clutch without any thought, but when you are learning you need to really focus on it each and every time. Seasoning is the same: the more you do it the more instinctive it becomes. When tasting always remember the golden rule, which is *never ever double dip*.

10. **Chill out, relax and enjoy the company.** This is my most important tip and I have left it to last. Remember, it's just a plate of food – the worst that can happen is you have to phone in a different plate of food.

Conversion charts

Oven temperatures

°C	Fan °C	°F	Gas
110	90	225	¼
130	110	250	½
140	120	275	1
150	130	300	2
160	140	325	3
180	160	350	4
190	170	375	5
200	180	400	6
220	200	425	7
230	210	450	8
240	220	475	9

Dry weights

Metric	Imperial	Metric	Imperial
5g	¼ oz	300g	11oz
15g	½ oz	350g	12oz
20g	¾ oz	375g	13oz
25g	1 oz	400g	14oz
40g	1½oz	425g	15oz
50g	2oz	450g	1lb
60g	2½oz	500g	1lb 2oz
75g	3oz	550g	1lb 3oz
100g	3½oz	600g	1lb 5oz
125g	4oz	650g	1lb 7oz
140g	4½oz	675g	1½lb
150g	5oz	700g	1lb 9oz
165g	5½oz	750g	1lb 11oz
175g	6oz	800g	1¾lb
200g	7oz	850g	1lb 14oz
225g	8oz	900g	2lb
250g	9oz	950g	2lb 2oz
275g	10oz	1kg	2lb 3oz

Liquid measures

Metric	Imperial	Aus	US
25ml	1fl oz		
50ml	2fl oz	¼ cup	¼ cup
75ml	3fl oz		
100ml	3½fl oz		
120ml	4fl oz	½ cup	½ cup
150ml	5fl oz		
175ml	6fl oz	¾ cup	¾ cup
200ml	7fl oz		
250ml	8fl oz	1 cup	1 cup
300ml	10fl oz	½ pint	1¼ cups
360ml	12fl oz		1½ cups
400ml	14fl oz		
450ml	16fl oz	2 cups	2 cups/ 1 US pint
600ml	1 pint	1 pint	2½ cups
750ml	1¼ pints		
900ml	1½ pints		3¾ cups
1 litre	1¾ pints	1¾ pints	1 quart

Recipe index

Gluten free

Vegetarian

Dairy free

Index

A

almonds
bakewell tart 257
with lamb tagine and bell peppers 83
with oven baked cannelloni, ricotta and butternut squash 123
with smoked trout, green salad, pea purée and dried cured ham 175

apple, and cinnamon scones 223

apricot, with belly of pork, set polenta, black pudding and spinach 127

arancini, with spicy Italian sausage 39

Arbroath smokie, potted, with oatcakes 35

asparagus
with hot smoked salmon pasta, fennel, broccoli and chilli 63
with pan seared mackerel, purple spouting broccoli and tomatoes 67

avocado, with Thai crab cakes and spiced mayonnaise 204

B

bacon
with mac 'n' cheese and leek 105
with pan roast chicken, cabbage, dauphinoise potatoes and French beans 119

beans
butter beans, with braised oxtail, vegetables and baby onions 131
cannellini beans, and pancetta soup 57
French beans
with pan roast chicken, cabbage and potatoes 119
with pan roast duck, potatoes and pancetta 169
with roast rump of lamb 115
mixed beans
with lamb shank and sundried tomatoes 135
with pan fried pork loin steak and chorizo 111

beef
braised with mashed potatoes and roasted roots 121
homemade pasta with meatballs in a spicy tomato sauce 61
peppered fillet with blue cheese, celery and walnut salad 179
rendang curry 96
steak pie 107

beetroot
with goats cheese, chutney and toasted hazelnuts 25
with pan seared breast of duck, cauliflower, kale and potatoes 165

berries
with cantaloupe melon 26
with passion fruit, lime and vanilla syrup 229
summer pudding 231

bhaji, onion 46

black pudding
with belly of pork, set polenta, spinach and apricots 127
with diced garlic potatoes and fried egg 31
with pan seared scallops, carrot purée and crispy shallots 29

bread
baked Camembert with red onion chutney 187
coriander, flat 152
focaccia 157
granary 153
Manchego-stuffed parcels 205
summer pudding 231

brownies, chocolate with cherry and walnut 243

C

cabbage
Chinese, spiced confit duck summer rolls 41
pickled, crispy Korean chicken wings with kimchi 43
red, braised pig's cheeks with mashed potatoes and pear 129
savoy
braised oxtail with vegetables, butter beans and onions 131
pan roast chicken with bacon, potatoes and French beans 119

seared monkfish with green vegetables and new potatoes 167
venison Wellington with new potatoes and baby carrots 185

carrot, cake 247

cauliflower, spiced and caramelised with duck, kale, beetroot and potatoes 165

cheese
blue cheese, salad with peppered fillet of beef 179
Camembert, baked with rosemary, hazelnut and red onion chutney 187
Cheddar
mac 'n' cheese with smoked bacon and leek 105
quiche with pancetta and leek 215
feta, with tomato lettuce cups and pomegranate 27
goats cheese
with salt pickled beetroot, chutney and toasted hazelnuts 25
with spring rolls and red pepper 38
Manchego
bread parcels stuffed with 205
chicken baked with Serrano ham, olives and pesto 113
mozzarella
with arancini, spicy Italian sausage and pine nuts 39
with pizza, chestnut mushrooms, red onion and chilli 198
with pizza, red chilli and basil pesto 202
paneer, with butternut squash, spicy onion, chilli and squash crisps 47
ricotta
oven baked cannelloni butternut squash and almonds 123
spinach tortellini with ham hock, tomato and chilli 197
sticky toffee pudding with figs and cinnamon 253

cheesecake
baked vanilla with cherry compote 238
chocolate and hazelnut 237

THANK YOU

This book has been created from over thirty years of cooking, teaching and learning. I would like to acknowledge the chefs who have made me the person I am today, and I would also like to thank the people who have helped me produce this book.

I have been very lucky in my career to have worked with some incredible people. My first job was probably the most crucial – the correct start and foundations are vital for any young chef. It was my brother who got me that start when I was fifteen years old; it was at a fantastic country house hotel where the chef Ian Knox took me under his wing. From there I moved to another amazing hotel with the most forward-thinking chef I have ever met: Pierre Giraud. He had systems set up almost thirty years ago that most kitchens are still trying to aspire to today.

The next chef who probably changed me the most was Ferrier Richardson. This was my first introduction to fine dining; his kitchens were very tough environments with very high standards. The pressure to perform was immense, but over the years he helped produce some of Scotland's best chefs.

I was then introduced to a chef called David Cowan; we ran a restaurant together, where it was just the two of us for a long time. I learned so much from David about food and how to have fun with it. We worked hard, but it was a brilliant learning experience.